Geo-Justice

A preferential option for the Earth

Drawing from his considerable experience in community organizing, education, and spiritual formation, James Conlon helps bridge the often divided worlds of those struggling for social justice and those seeking a creation centred spirituality. The name he gives this converging terrain is "Geo-Justice." As both a spiritual vision and a framework for political action, Geo-Justice seeks to heal the brokenness and make whole the relationships of humans with the Earth, with each other, and within our psyches. Conlon integrates the liberation and empowerment approaches of people like Saul Alinsky on the one hand, and the creation-oriented perspectives of Matthew Fox and Thomas Berry on the other, showing both approaches are integral to human development and saving the planet. Each chapter is followed by exercises that help readers map and develop their own journeys in Geo-Justice. This is an excellent guide for both reflection and action, spiritual growth and practical outreach in Geo-Justice.

Patricia Mische

Co-Founder, Global Education Associates
Author of *Star Wars and the State of our Souls: Deciding the Future of Planet Earth*

Geo-Justice

A preferential option for the Earth

by James Conlon

Wood Lake Books
Inc

Resource
Publications, Inc.

Cover photo courtesy of NASA.

Canadian Cataloguing in Publication Data

Conlon, James A., 1936–

    Geo-Justice

    ISBN 0–919599–89–3

    I. Human ecology — Religious aspects —

Christianity. I. Title

BT695.5.C65 1990   261.8'362   C90–091194–8

**U. S. Library of Congress
Cataloging in Publication Data**

ISBN 0-89390-182-2

available from Resource Publications, Inc.

160 East Virginia Street, #290, San Jose, CA 95112.

Published by

Wood Lake Books Inc.,   **Resource Publications, Inc.**

Box 700, Winfield, BC,   160 East Virginia St., #290

Canada V0H 2C0   San Jose, CA, USA 95112

Printed in Canada by

Hignell Printing Ltd.,

Winnipeg, MB, R3G 2B4

Table of Contents

Acknowledgements

Gratitude is about acknowledging what we have received as gifts; it is a declaration of the interconnectedness that has shaped our origins and configures our future. The composition of these pages has been for me such a gift. The gifts flow from many sources for which I express my thanks.

• To the rivers, oceans, land and sky that continually ignite and reveal deep sources of the Earth's wisdom.

• To Richard and Elizabeth, my parents, who gave me life and love.

• To Margaret and Clarice, who were so special in my life.

• To Bob and Mary, my brother and sister, who have encouraged me in this project as in other undertakings.

• To my ancestors, my collaborators from my Canadian homeland, my mentors, colleagues, students, and friends with whom I have been privileged to celebrate shared wisdom and to wonder together about justice-making in and through the earth.

• To those compassionate co-adventurers, many of whose words and names appear in the pages of this book, with whom I have journeyed into Geo-Justice through a quest for communion, through the discovery of uniqueness, through the honoring of the inner voice. Among these, I owe particular thanks to Jack Egan and Matthew Fox.

• To Peter Reynolds, Cathryn Farrell, Linda Sewright, the late Donna Mattern, and Marilyn Goddard, who worked with me on the text.

• To Jim Taylor of Wood Lake Books, and Ken Guentert of Resource Publications, who have been most helpful in bringing this manuscript to publication.

Finally, my thanks to you readers who join all of these I have mentioned on the adventure of living from the perspective of a living Earth. Welcome. May our journey continue.

Foreword

by Thomas Berry

This book by James Conlon might be considered something of a flowering of the ecology movement which began with Rachel Carson's *Silent Spring,* published in 1962. Since then an ever-increasing transformation of human consciousness has been taking place. It is the most significant transformation movement, perhaps, since the beginning of civilization.

Some 5,000 years ago, humans began putting stress upon the natural world that has culminated in the industrial assault on the planet in these past two centuries. This final assault originated in the western European world, then extended to North America and throughout the planet. Its most obvious example is the petrochemical industry of the post-war period, an industry that has multiplied itself and is now in its most virulent phase.

Resistance to the disturbed relations between humans and the Earth was begun in the 19th century, but this movement was overwhelmed by the power of the commercial-industrial enterprise, and by the mystique of "progress" that has pervaded all our thinking, our education, and our sense of reality and value. But now, finally, after *Silent Spring*, a tide of opposition has arisen. Our industrial "progress" is now recognized as a deep cultural pathology that has poisoned our environment and given us a grimy world.

The Ecology Movement began a profound cultural therapy. It seeks not the exploitation of the Earth but a mutually enhancing human presence on the Earth. This movement is guided by an awareness that the universe is a communion of subjects, not a collection of objects. But if this is true of the universe, it is infinitely more true of the Earth in its myriad expressions of geological, biological, and human modes of being and acting.

For too long we have been autistic in relation to the natural world. We did not hear the voices, we did not experience the exaltation of speaking and listening to the mountains, the rivers, the meadows, the birds, the cicadas and crickets on summer evenings. It was all lovely enough, entrancing as the sea in all its power and

7

majesty as we walk along the shore. But all these experiences were trivial in their impact on human consciousness; they did not prevent us from our ever-increasing devastation.

Finally, however, we have entered on a new period. Naturalists such as a Loren Eiseley have restored the natural history essay that had such wonderful expression in the 19th century. The archetypal figures will always be Henry Thoreau and John Muir, but new writers such as Peter Matthiesson, Farley Mowat, David Raines Wallace, Scott Momaday, Barry Lopez and Annie Dillard, and poets such as Gary Snyder and Wendell Berry, now present us with remarkable insight the experiences of the plant and animal realms. Such writers are joined by scientists and others on ecological issues—along with an extensive array of publications from eco-feminists, religious authors, and those concerned with ethical aspects of the environmental issue.

Within this context, we can see this book on Geo-Justice as a flowering of the entire movement.

The full power of ecology can only be felt in the realization that the universe, the planet Earth, and all living and non-living beings exist primarily for celebration. The universe is a single, vast, celebratory event! Here the poetry, the music, the mystique of the Earth—all find expression. Just as the earliest of the natural history writers were inspired by the romantic tradition of the later 18th century and the beginning of the 19th century, so now after a period of "realism" that had no place for the more numinous qualities of the universe we are able once again to hear the music and experience the depth of fulfillment that are available to us, once we are attuned to the symphony of voices around us.

Thomas Berry
Author of *The Dream of the Earth*

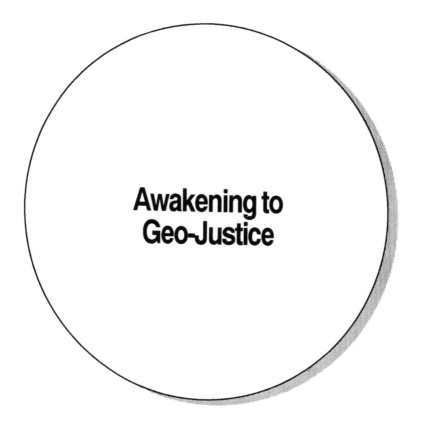

Awakening to Geo-Justice

The genesis of Geo-Justice

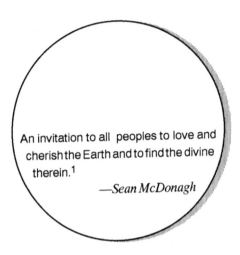

An invitation to all peoples to love and cherish the Earth and to find the divine therein.[1]

—*Sean McDonagh*

Geo-Justice—A Preferential Option for the Earth represents my personal journey over more than two decades. This journey has led me through pastoral work, therapy, community organization, theological education and spirituality. It has taken me from the street to the classroom and back.

This is more than my own journey, for it also documents the cultural shifts and awakenings of our era. We are, I believe, seeing a new awareness, a new understanding of "cherishing the earth and finding the divine therein."

In this book, I invite you, too, on a journey.

The journey begins with a new vision of justice—a "preferential option for the Earth." It indicates how bringing the "geo" into the justice-making activities of our culture and society can bring us into harmony with nature, transforming our approach to the planet, the local community, and ourselves.

To live a preferential option for the Earth is to view our time within the context of the Paschal mystery. As a theological perspective, it integrates and celebrates today's events and trends as a profound enactment of the Crucifixion, Resurrection, and Pentecost events in our time. As René Dubois' book *A God Within* points out, the Paschal mystery is woven into the very fabric of the Earth's existence:

The eternal movement from life to dead organic substance, …to simple chemical molecules which are converted back into plant and animal life again, is a physical manifestation of the myth of eternal return.[2]

This theology sees the cross in the death of tropical rain forests in Brazil; in the struggles of marginalized black people in Harlem; in toxic chemicals in our food, water, and air; in the collapse of leadership and political systems in Eastern Europe, in China, in South Africa; in the erosion of our cultural soul by drug abuse; in the tragedy of AIDS…

These and other indicators are the crucifixion of the "mystical body of the Earth." They are a cosmic Crucifixion—in which dying becomes a transforming act.

Like a planetary earthquake, the crises currently endangering our planet shake our understanding of who we are, and why we are here. We live simultaneously in a time of breakdown and break-through. The major diseases of our time offer an analogy for seeing how these devastating events ultimately point us toward harmony, balance and peace. Those who are fascinated by the vision of Geo-Justice become hospice workers for an era that is dying, and midwives for an era about to be born.

The personal implications of this crisis point to a spiritual opportunity. With this in mind, I discuss several approaches for finding our proper place in the work of Geo-Justice on this planet.

Be patient with all that is unsolved in your heart. Try to love the questions themselves like locked rooms and like books that are written in a foreign tongue… Live the questions…[3]
—*Rainer Maria Rilke*

11

What is Geo-Justice?

I approach Geo-Justice as a question to be lived. Like electricity, which we can only identify by its effects on other things—light bulbs and meters, stoves and motors, transistors and microchips—I describe the effect that Geo-Justice has on people caught by its vision.

New life, the surprise of Resurrection, is inexorably connected to the cross. In the death of the old lies the possibility of the new.

Geo-Justice is, therefore, about liberating the Earth from all that oppresses it. This liberation unleashes our latent possibilities; efforts toward self-actualization become mini-Resurrections. These expressions of new life offer signs of hope within the events of our time.

Listening to these signs of hope, we surrender into action. Our responses call us into personal deaths—death to our isolation from self and from Earth; to a mechanistic world view; to a tired understanding of justice that promotes resignation, despair, and misguided anger...

In this book, I reflect on the meaning of death, and its significance for the Earth. We mourn and lament the Earth's pain; we feel outrage at the violence perpetrated upon our planet; we undergo a profound shift of consciousness. Resurrection is never to what was, but to what will be. It is always unexpected, always a surprise. The surprise of Geo-Justice is a new and expanded perspective on life. In the experience of union with ultimate reality, we discover new delight in the rhythm of ocean waves, the caress of an evening breeze, the rich promise of a plowed field. Human life is part of this tapestry of gratitude—be it the support of a loved one, the urge for human rights, the joy of a newborn child, or the grace of racial and sexual equality.

Geo-Justice has three components.

• The **Global** component invites us to experience the Earth as a whole.

• The **Local** component enables us to see our concrete actions as manifestations of the divine presence.

• The **Psycho-Social** component affirms a congruence between our personal journeys and the great issues of our time; the psyche functions as a microcosm of the universe.

As a "Window for the World," Geo-Justice invites us to see the world in a new way. In the Paschal mystery, death and new life are woven together, into a tapestry of ecological health and harmonic social justice. Geo-Justice becomes an operative vision for creating harmony and balance on the Earth, in our community, and within ourselves.

The Paschal mystery story culminates in the Pentecost event. Pentecost unites what had been separated; it offers healing for wounds. In Geo-Justice, a planetary Pentecost calls forth the birth of a new Earth, a new people, a new creation.

Through the lens of Geo-Justice, we view the events of these concluding years of the millennium as a profound reenactment of the Paschal mystery; we move from cherishing the divine presence in the earth, through the cosmic Crucifixion of ecological devastation and social injustice, to the empty tomb of mysticism, of prophecy, of deep motivation, culminating in the hope of new life in a Pentecost for the planet.

Making our Easter: a work of the heart

Justice—peace with the Earth—implies a transformation of people and of society.

This work of justice will be a work of the heart—a falling in love with the divine voice that summons us to listen and to become one with the oppressed Earth. Passion and compassion for the Earth become the new vision for our time, a vision that brings new energy to the work of restoring ecological devastation and of relieving psychic, social, and global oppression.

Paulo Freire, the Brazilian educator, describes his work of liberating the oppressed as "making my Easter."[4] The work of Geo-Justice involves "making Easter" by liberating every species, every human, and the Earth itself.

13

Part I

The Earth's story for our time

The vision of Geo-Justice

Above all, where there is no vision we lose the sense of our greater power to transcend history and create a new future for ourselves with others... Therefore the quest is not a luxury; life itself demands it of us![5]

—*Vincent Harding*

More and more, people are awakening to their responsibility for healing the wounds of our Earth. In all parts of the planet, individuals and groups share a common vision. They give each other the support, and provide the information needed, to bring harmony and balance to the life systems and cultural relationships on the Earth.

As they reflect on their personal stories, they stand in awe of the beauty that surrounds them. They are nourished by the promise that the world can be whole and healthy again.

These people feel called to heal and to be healed, to bring together fractured relationships and to dissolve their sense of separation from the Earth. They hear the voice of the child within; they see themselves as a microcosm of the universe at peace. They rejoice at how much more there is to know, to celebrate, to savor. They are companions for each other on the journey.

These people yearn to become what they were meant to be—to live from their hearts, to express their true nature, to heal each other, to bring balance and harmony to the Earth. This yearning generates fresh energy for communication, for connectedness.

Themes of healing and transformation invite these people to the

15

"What's next?" of their lives. To this question, people bring a rich diversity of experience and background. Sexual minorities, spiritual psychologists, authors, leaders of study groups, dancers, artists, drama teachers, peace and justice workers, liturgists, musicians, engineers, economists, organizers, theologians and others—all engage in discerning and healing the wounds of our lives, our culture, our world. Thus a communion of compassion grows into communities of deeper meaning and purpose. Educators and activists, concerned about peace, use storytelling as a vehicle of non-violence. Church people find ways of integrating theology and practice. More and more people—be they men or women, gay, lesbian, or straight, of any race, age, or social status—find healing and friendship in their relationships with each other and with the Earth.

People are converging, in fact, to create a possible future.

In their belonging to this vast, growing, yet-to-be-defined movement, people become children again. They dance and sing, celebrate differences, and make justice an act of love. In business, politics, education, or any other cultural contribution, they are committed to a fresh and deeper life that both honors their experiences and frees them from conformity. They are convinced that they are born in blessing, invited to be instruments of peace.

Their response to this banquet of beauty is to engage in a cultural renaissance for the new millennium. They share resources—written, recorded and personal—to encourage a spiritual awakening, to restore the environment, and to heal the wounds of racism, sexism, and economic imbalance.

Among these people, base groups are emerging, communities for environmental, personal, local, and global concerns. These concerns are often expressed through images and metaphors, and break through into celebrations of ritual and roots.

As communities from diverse places make contact with each other, they discover that their visions and actions have not occurred in isolation; they are part of a movement for peace with the Earth. They discover in their movement a oneness with all of creation.

These people, these groups, have discovered a language, a process, an operative myth for balance and harmony on the planet; they have discovered Geo-Justice.

> Humankind has suddenly entered into a brand new relationship with our planet. Unless we quickly and profoundly change the course of our civilization, we face an immediate and grave danger of destroying the world-wide ecological system that sustains life as we know it.[6]
>
> —*Albert Gore Jr.*

A communion of justice-makers

There are many wonderful and effective projects for justice-making and social change on our planet. But it is also true that the work for justice has fallen on hard times. In my experience, many people find justice-making "glum plodding." Their work feels abstract, unconnected. It is full of obligation; it lacks excitement, creativity, energy, and deep satisfaction.

Let me offer a diagnosis of the problem. Until now, justice work in our culture and our churches has lacked a connection with the Earth. In his book *The Culture of Narcissism*, Christopher Lasch points out that we live in a society where preoccupation with self and introspection is a dominant trend. This view is underlined by Robert Bellah and his colleagues who, in *Habits of the Heart: Individualism and Commitment in American Life*, assert that we live in an ethos of individualism, where preoccupation with personal healing far outweighs concerns for systemic change and transformation.

In this book, I propose that justice in and through the Earth implies a transformation of people and of society. Like a hologram, in which any part of the picture can generate the whole image, each individual person represents all of society and the Earth. Therefore we must work to transform all levels—personal, local, societal, global—interdependently and simultaneously.

Geo-Justice re-visions justice-making. In our time, cultural and ecclesial organizations strive to bring about justice for whales, for forests, for battered wives and abused children, for the poor, for victims of oppression... All these causes are worthy. Yet most of these efforts remain fragmented, isolated from each other.

Liberation theology has helped us to recognize the poor and oppressed as a primary source of divine presence and revelation. Extending that recognition, we can also begin to see in our present history of cultural collapse and ecological devastation the oppressed Earth itself as a source of divine wisdom for our actions.

In her book *Beyond Mere Obedience*, theologian Dorothee Soelle reminds us that the power to change things rests in our capacity for spontaneity. We need not be constrained by the present. Such a spontaneity invites us to respond to the oppression of people and of the Earth by forming coalitions to liberate powers presently unexpressed in self and society.

Justice with the earth will be a work of the heart—a falling in love with the divine voice that summons us to become one with the beautiful and oppressed Earth.

Geo-Justice will be more a participation than an obligation— more about love than about laws, more about harmony than have-to's. Geo-Justice extends the compassion of the heart into the psyche, society, and Earth. It is about healing ourselves, our systems, and our planet.

Geo-Justice will liberate the poor, and liberate our poor Earth. It is a preferential option for the Earth.

Myths bring energy to people, shaping their perceptions, unifying their vision. To restore our present ecological devastation, to bring liberation to our psyche, society, and globe we need a new myth.

Geo-Justice is an operative myth for our time.

Justice for the Earth
The old order is dying and a new one is being born. This is the Paschal mystery, in which death promises and reveals resurrection.

Such a moment releases enormous energy for transformation. In it, we see our personal story as intimately connected to the story of the universe.

Geo-Justice is a preferential option promising justice for the whole Earth. In this perspective, no significant decision or action occurs without assessing how that action or decision would affect the Earth.

> Strong forces of encapsulation
> Surroundings of belief
> Collapse into a deeper sense of truth,
> Evolving a cosmic concern for Earth.

> GAIA, Geo, Mother, Jewel,
> You are the source of life and strength;
> You are the metaphor of fact and continuity
> Animating and alluring
> Trust in peace.

—Conlon

At this crucial moment in the Earth's history, we are invited to be collaborators, co-workers and friends of the Earth. Thomas Berry says, "We are as much a part of Earth as the rocks, the water and the air."[7] At certain times, we sense that unity with the Earth. The darkness of the sea, of the night sky, of our own soul—these are places where we feel ourselves hovering on the edge of new beginnings, new understandings, new responses.

For the Dene nation of Canada's North West Territories, theEarth is a living reality that fashions their psychology and their very identity. To them, fishing is as much a spiritual activity as an economic one. The land reminds them of the unity of all of life. They say: "The grass, the trees, the animals are our flesh... (the land) is just like a mother to us... it is my teacher... it belongs to the unborn... we respect the ways of the land as if it were a person."[8]

> The greatest beauty
> is organic wholeness,
> the wholeness of life and things,
> the divine beauty of the universe.
> Love that, not man apart from
> that...[9]
> *—Robinson Jeffers*

In the act of creativity, we celebrate divinity. As Meister Eckhart, the 14th-century theologian, wrote, "The seed of God is in us... a seed of God grows into God." In our moments of creativity, we know a unity with the world around us. Our creativity draws on a reservoir of universal consciousness; we know that we belong to all of life, in all its many forms. We are citizens of a planet full of life, people of promise and agents of surprise.

Instinctively, we reach for our roots, seeking our oneness with the Earth. Not long ago, I retraced the steps of my ancestors in south and central Ontario, in Canada. I visited the farms, cemeteries and remaining relatives of my French and Irish forebears. Traveling with my sister, I took from each grave site and farm a sample of the earth. At the end of the trip, I placed some of this soil in a small jar, and labeled it "Jim's Bioregional Earth." Because that is, literally, the earth from which I come.

We all come from the same Earth. We who live on this planet are united in this matter, this *mater*, Mother and Father, that is the unifying source of our being.

Our common heritage and source remind us that we can be co-workers for Geo-Justice on our planet. In developing the concept of Geo-Justice, I find increasingly that Geo-Justice is about celebrating harmony and healing in and of the Earth; it is a holistic approach rooted in the Earth itself. Geo-Justice seeks a resonance with the divine and with creation that will enable us to enter the new millennium and achieve a place of peace.

Geo-Justice does not lend itself to the limits of a definition. Geo-Justice is a vision, a language, a metaphor, an operative myth. It is an approach to healing the wounds of the Earth, a process for generating balance and harmony on the planet.

It operates through the healing energy of global mysticism, and through prophetic work that both seeks and proclaims divine action in the world. As we discover our destiny, we are transformed; we see and act toward the Earth in a new way. Our energies attune to this work as a tuning fork sings when it picks up the vibrations around it.

Geo-Justice reminds us that we *are* the Earth; we are not separate from the planet. In Geo-Justice seminars, I invite participants to become personally, culturally and globally aware of the

20

dynamics of the universe, and to celebrate deeply their connection with the Earth. One such seminar offered these metaphors:

- I'm greening in harmony.
- I'm the heart of the Earth; the Earth beats in me.
- One cell, one people, one heart, one universe.
- Birthing a new social order.
- The cry of the oppressed earth.

The invitation

As the old order gives way, a new order is about to be born. What happened at Pentecost, a time of transformation some 20 centuries ago, is, I believe, deepening and expanding today.

At this time, our culture needs a hospice, a context in which old understandings and social structures may break down and die. At the same time, we need to be midwives to provide energy and support for the breakthrough of the new cultural genesis being born.

We are invited in this moment to become instruments of Geo-Justice and architects of a planetary Pentecost. I am convinced that the path to a planetary Pentecost calls for a convergence of our collective energies. It is nothing less than an invitation to be a new people in a new millennium. This invitation is as strong as a gravitational pull. I call it a "magnetic intuition." It calls forth that which is deepest, most fascinating and most wonderful to us, and invites us to respond.

The movement toward breakthrough, toward becoming who we are, is for me very like spring. As René Dubois noted in *A God Within*, "To experience a spring day is enough to assure me that eventually life will triumph over death."[10] Springtime bursts upon us with a new openness, a rush of harmony and balance on the Earth. Spring invites us to participate in new life. Geo-Justice invites us to participate in a new Earth. Like spring, the conviction that a new era is upon us deepens our awareness of our experiences. Life is both joy and pain. We know that we are not whole until we have dealt with and celebrated both.

The mystical awareness of being in touch with a common source of energy that runs through all things constantly reminds us of our connections to the cosmos. Geo-Justice invites us to develop our lives in harmony with the life processes of the planet. We adopt a prophetic view which trusts that the Earth is good, that we are all equal and that the divine permeates all things, including ourselves. In Geo-Justice, we are invited to become instruments of planetary healing, connecting our own joy and pain to the Earth's.

It's a challenging position, walking on the hot coals of a dying culture even as we celebrate the first cries of new life. But that is what we are invited to do. As the late poet bp Nicol put it, in a mantra sung at a Thanksgiving banquet in Toronto, Canada:

"If we're here for anything at all
It's to take care of the Earth."

A new soul for justice-making

The Earth is a living mandala—a structural matrix through and from which flow a succession of changes, elemental forms, and primal surges, each surpassing the other in an infinite variety of organic structures and impulses, crowned by the supreme attribute of reflective consciousness.[11]

—José and Miriam Argüelles

Much of my adult life I have wondered about questions of justice. As an organizer, pastoral worker, therapist and educator, the questions continue to challenge me. What is justice? What do we do about it? What does the doing mean anyway?

Experience teaches us that efforts toward justice and peace are often unsuccessful. Tenants win a victory, only to lose their building. Unions negotiate improved conditions, only to see their plant moved to a developing country. Human rights efforts succumb to famine and economic crisis.

Unsuccessful programs nudge people to the threshold of despair. Overwhelmed and confused, many no longer believe that their efforts will ever make any real difference. My experience of more than two decades testifies that justice work is often more a conceptual obligation than a passionate channel of collaboration and engagement.

Yet in the midst of such resignation, recent developments in science reveal that the universe is designed for balance, for harmony, for interdependence—that is, for justice. Harmony is coded into the universe. Our work, then, is to participate in that harmony, to change the ways in which we humans have interrupted the balance of the Earth's processes.

José and Miriam Argüelles, in their book *Mandala*, suggest that the Earth is a living mandala.[12] Carl Jung wrote of the meaning of a mandala: "It... serves the creative purpose of giving expression and form to something that does not yet exist, something new and unique."[13] From this perspective of the Earth as a mandala, an integration of individual consciousness and global awareness can come into being—we re-vision justice-making and become workers for Geo-Justice, shapers of a planetary Pentecost where hope and compassion can replace abstraction and despair.

In the work of Geo-Justice, we become aware that justice is ultimately the work of the universe, and that our work is to become conscious participants in that event—described by Argüelles as, "...a succession of changes, elemental forms, and primal surges ... crowned by the supreme attribute of reflective consciousness."[14]

An attitude for liberation

Nothing illustrates better for me the nature of Geo-Justice than a child named Julian. He was born in May 1986 in the Central American country of Honduras, a cradle of poverty and political strife. Julian was adopted by a wonderful Canadian couple. In their kitchen hangs a plaque: "Never forget for a moment, you didn't grow under my heart, but in it."

Julian has never read Meister Eckhart, but his entire being declares Eckhart's theology: "Now the moment I flowed out from the Creator all creatures shouted: 'Behold, here is God!'"[15]

Julian's approach to life is loving and inclusive. He celebrates every moment of his existence. I asked his mother what being his mother meant to her. "To understand the depth and joy of how he sees life," she replied. Julian sees every moment as an adventure. A trip to the park, watching *Sesame Street,* or an encounter with his puppies—he greets each option of living with ecstasy and engagement. He bases his choices on a deep trust in his parents, his sister Laura, his puppies and those who delight in who he is.

His father says that every day with Julian is a discovery of what life is about, an adventure with an energy that unifies and celebrates. Julian celebrates the moment in unselfconscious joy; he allows

24

surprises to be part of his very being. He truly affirms the gospel invitation to become as little children; his life is a constant invitation to be a child like him.

I have another young friend, named Jamie. A different but equally true plaque hangs in his home. It says: "There are two lasting gifts we can give our children. One is roots and the other wings." When Julian's mother read those words, she agreed: "Yes, you give them a foundation, and then you let them go." As another old saying goes: "You give them life, you give them love, you give them up."

The folk wisdom about "roots" and "wings" expresses Julian's direction and development. Julian has taught me much about life. I thank him for being my teacher in Geo-Justice.

Geo-Justice starts as an attitude, an awareness. It is an avenue of liberation for the voiceless and the oppressed. Consider these words, for example, written by Oscar, a federal prisoner in Ashland, Kentucky. They reflect a deep appreciation of the creative energy that permeates all of life.

> Like bells made beautiful
> In different sound and harmonies
> We can do the same with our lives.
> With unquenchable fervent like fire
> When we grow in the understanding
> of the wisdom of God,
> Then we find more and more
> Our lives are filled with joyful hearing
> Concerning ourselves and others.

Oscar wrote those words at a retreat. An older man at the same retreat wrote,

> My dad was a violent man.
> They told me I was a good boy.
> When my father was not at home,
> and when I was lonely,
> I went out to see the stars and the moon,
> And I wasn't lonely anymore.

When I read that, I knew I was in the presence of a mystic, a person who experienced unity with the divine.

In that workshop/retreat with Oscar and 20 others, I learned again that good things can happen in jail. Some of history's most powerful words have been written in prison—by Dietrich Bonhoeffer, John of the Cross, Martin Luther King Jr., Dorothy Day, John Bunyan, Saul Alinsky and others. In a sense, all of us are doing time in the cellblocks of our psyches and the confines of our culture. Geo-Justice offers an avenue of liberation for each of us.

When those inmates in Kentucky beat on drums together and ritualized their pain, the liberating power for a spiritual awakening came from their wounds. Carlos described the drum as a microcosm of the rhythm and energy of the universe.

Another inmate, Tim, wrote a verse for a song for the closing ritual: "And something came over me/And said I could be free..." A man called Ed wrote, "Mystery creates us, mystery sustains us. It's about snow-capped mountains melting into the ocean. I don't know why my heart beats, but it does."

A few days later, Tim wrote in a letter: "I have finished the day working in the aftermath of this weekend—I have found that since I slayed my dragon, I am full of energy. I woke up to my spirit." Tim recognized Geo-Justice as an awakening of the spirit, a discovery of our relationship with the cosmos which frees us from helplessness and despair.

It was of this that Thomas Merton said: "I exist under trees, I walk in the woods out of necessity. I am both a prisoner and an escaped prisoner... I know there are trees here. I know there are birds here... I share this particular place with them: we form an ecological balance."[16]

Gender harmony

The drum beaten by the inmates in their ritual is a symbol. It sounds the pulse of our destiny and direction; it is the heartbeat, the call to life. Often, we fear that pulsing rhythm. It arouses our vitality. In music, in dance, the drum drives us to be men and women with blood coursing through our veins. It stimulates us to be people of passion, of transformation. The energy of the drum has its source in the universe.

Our sexuality can be a source of and a force for transformation.

Awareness of this possibility invites men and women to see their individual journeys as a common journey, a cultural event that is both feminist and pro-male. Myths, metaphors, and rituals unite into a fully embodied sexuality that is both heroic and adventurous. When we explore femininity and masculinity deeply, we discover opportunities for union that transcend our differences.

Gender not only clarifies who we are, but illuminates what we can become together. Gender harmony symbolizes the planetary peace we seek.

To speak of the opposite sex is to distort the intent of our sexuality. We need each other; we cannot do without each other. Our sexuality energizes our relationship with the whole of creation—we need each other in our global journey toward Geo-Justice.

Too often, sexuality is treated as a source of guilt, rather than of mysticism and compassion. Sex becomes a means of gaining power *over* the other. But for men—and I believe for women—sexuality offers a gender-based source of passion and power *within*.

As a man, I can assert that when I dig deeply into the hidden recesses of my psyche, I find there a new source of power that is neither "macho" nor "wimp" but a dialectical strength that is both strong and gentle, full and empty, creative and receptive, dynamic and liberating, compassionate and stubborn, prophetic and embracing of peace.

The work of transformation starts, for many, with gender justice. Currently, our churches and our society are developing new images of gender. From inclusive language to equal-pay legislation, we are encouraged to treat sexuality in a new way.

Our gender roles reflect one aspect of the changes bubbling up in our culture—the old ways are dying, and new relationships are being born. Sexuality is a beginning point, a revelation of the nature of Geo-Justice. It reminds us of the diversity and generativity on the Earth.

The birth of feminism is a deep cultural rite of passage in the development of a civilization attuned to the dynamics of the universe. It liberates us from the prisons of ancient preconceptions into a new Earth community that seeks to live in cooperation and interdependence with all life systems on the planet.

The power of the universe

Deep within the recesses of our being, striving for expression, for recognition and strength, a generative force emerges. Often we do not know what to call it; we simply know it is there. Sometimes we become aware of it. Dr. Robert McClure, the Canadian medical missionary who served at great personal risk in four war zones, once described it as "A hand in the middle of your back, pushing you on!"

This force, once acknowledged, will not be denied. It cries out for expression; it demands release and liberation. From it arises a conviction not to be repressed. This force pays little attention to so-called common sense. It responds in compassion when it sees innocent children starving in Ethiopia; it rises in anger when urban gangs rape a jogger in New York. It knows, beyond any argument or debate, that this world is not how it should be. In the emptying and release that accompanies that acknowledgment, newness emerges from nothingness, appearance from emptiness, cohesion from chaos, and courage from fear. We are simultaneously transformed and transformers.

This profound and irrepressible generative force identifies the latent strength of Geo-Justice. For if Geo-Justice concerns our oneness with the universe, then such a force can be nothing more than the power of the universe welling up within us, speaking through us. Here creativity and unpredictability coincide.

Here the vision of Geo-Justice takes shape. It is a harmony and balance that finds embodiment in the child and opportunity behind bars. It is demonstrated in the diversity of gender and expressed in a passion for peace. It reaches its collective culmination in the coalition of a new soul for justice-making.

Peace with the Earth

In an ideal world peace would be more than a lull between wars—it would be an accepted state of mind, a way of life, a firm principle shaping the behavior of individuals, families and societies and their relationships with each other, and...with all other living things and with the Earth itself.[17]

—*Peace Conference, Costa Rica*

The announcement above opened a meeting in San Jose, Costa Rica, attended by 700 people from around the world. They gathered in response to the invitation of the late mythologist Joseph Campbell, who proposed planet Earth as the unifying myth for our time. From Bahai to Buddhist, Quaker to Christian, Native to New Age, European to American, Costa Rican to Canadian—and from the Dalai Lama to the Archbishop—people came from all corners and all faiths of the world for one purpose: to remember our interconnectedness and the fragile state of the Earth.

We came together to focus on the theme, "Seeking the True Meaning of Peace." Aware that "the severity of the threat to the biosphere is replacing the threat of nuclear war as the major threat to human survival,"[18] we set as our goal nothing less than the transformation of ecological devastation and negative national relationships into planetary and personal peace.

As we gathered, we were all conscious that deep mystical traditions united us. This unity wove a tapestry of kindness to alter the torn fabric of violence evident in many places of the world—a kindness that appeared as compassionate energy.

29

A vision of a common future emerged. A vision of peace healed our separateness and energized a spirit of oneness. The illusion of separateness from self, each other, or creation, began to collapse. Our common connection to the Earth made us all citizens of the same planet. This awareness of oneness with the planet allowed healing responses to come forth.

Such a conference is a beginning. The result of such visioning will eventually be new social forms organizing themselves into a new global civilization. These forms will transcend the historic political and ideological bounds of nations. This emerging civilization will acknowledge differences without comparing them. It will value gifts without competing, and will share a common vision of the future, as one family for a better world.

The experience of peace also evokes gratitude for all of creation. In an absence of the aggression that presently permeates people, family, community, nation and Earth, we can reverence the woods, the sea, the air as the sources of what is precious and important for life.

Peace on Earth

People at that conference affirmed that there can be no peace on Earth without peace with the Earth. They identified some characteristics of that peace:

- **democracy** as participation in a dignified manner with all life forms;
- **disarmament** as the acknowledgment of the basic needs of all expressions of life;
- **debt resolution** as the restoration of a people's collective soul;
- **protection against deforestation** as a compassionate response to the life systems of the environment, the very lungs of this Earth;
- **abolition of drug abuse** as the promotion of psychic balance for people on the planet.

In these characteristics, economy and ecology merge. New structures of global responsibility restore harmony between people and nature. Our common future for a better world will be built out of mutual sensitivity and vulnerability.

When we gratefully acknowledge the universe as our home, we collectively give birth to a new vision of peace. The *Declaration of Human Responsibilities for Peace and Sustainable Development* underlines this approach:

Everything that exists is part of the unfolding of an interdependent universe.

Life on Earth is abundant and diverse.

Of all living beings, humans have the unique capacity to decide consciously whether to protect or damage the quality and conditions of life on Earth.[19]

Commitment to peace

The Earth was not created for people, but people were created for the Earth. You have probably heard the saying: "Think globally and act locally." Robert Muller of the United Nations has rephrased that prophetically: "We need to think cosmologically, and act globally and locally."[20] Our cooperative actions for peace, though diverse in expression, will send ripples for peace throughout the planet. Out of a sense of responsibility for a peaceful future, we will celebrate the sacredness of all life. A Bri Bri native teacher of Costa Rica proclaimed this truth during the conference: "We share the same sky, same sun, same river; we are all one."

Understanding this unity will call forth an awareness of our common roots and of the presence of the divine in all things. We will see that all humans must share in healing our current sense of separateness from the Earth.

Archetypal psychologist Jean Bolen compares this cultural moment to the time just before birth when there is an irreversible commitment to whatever happens. As people of peace, our commitment to this time is to make wisdom possible; to experience love and beauty; to participate in the unfolding consciousness of the planet as a living being. In this period of extraordinary change, we celebrate that everything is part of everything else on the Earth.

So we search for a strategy to help us move from ambivalence to ecological commitment. We seek a strategy that is effective, liberating and appropriate for the magnitude of the issues that confront us. The awareness that an increasing number of people share this view provides encouragement.

Energy for peace will be focused through participation in base groups. Base groups, or base communities, have been the means of revitalizing the church in Latin America and in many other parts of the world. They will do the same for peace with the Earth. Such base groups can be a vehicle for generating a critical mass of people moving from separation to oneness and empowerment.

As groups link together, a growing number of peacemakers will discover increased harmony within, and balance without. Because the base groups themselves will be inclusive and non-hierarchical, cultures of violence will change to non-violence.

Global citizen Thomas Paine is reputed to have said, "The world is my country, to do good is my religion." This is the hope for base groups of peace.

The rights of the Earth

Peace is an essential dimension of Geo-Justice. Peacemakers take it upon themselves to remain open to life and available to surprise. They receive everything as given and trust the giver. They express their interdependence with all that they receive. They see and celebrate peace with the Earth as a gift of Geo-Justice.

My friends Filberto and Martha are examples of peacemakers. They live in Costa Rica, a country without an army and the setting for the United Nations University for Peace. For them, life is most profoundly possible when we receive everything as a gift. To live simply, with hospitality and love, is the deepest experience of life— to share all we have, and to acknowledge gratefully that whatever we receive connects us to all life. With this attitude, peace is possible and Geo-Justice is alive among us.

Geo-Justice is not a single program which others must follow. Rather, it celebrates and depends on the diversity of each of our expressions of healing and compassion.

Geo-Justice draws together a coalition of people sharing a common vision, working out day by day a new configuration of energy for our culture, our planet and ourselves. This coalition finds its focus in the image of "roots and wings"—like the plaque in Jamie's home. Roots invite us to mine our traditions and our origins, to find within them the stories and the strengths that keep us going even when success seems unattainable. Wings summon us to soar, to see visions and to dream dreams, to seek personal and political frontiers as yet unattained.

To participate in such a coalition, our unique contribution to Geo-Justice must start with who we are and what we do right now. Our surrounding culture, like a huge computer, strives to program every action and direction of our lives. It wants to shape us to what we are not. By being and acting who we are, we are liberated from this oppression.

Geo-Justice is about healing the separations in our lives and on the Earth. We have too much separation—between personal and political, body and body politic, generativity and the ability to act, mysticism and global perspectives, prophecy and local action, self-knowledge and social awareness. Coming together to build a new soul will move us toward the global event, a planetary Pentecost, the advent of a new kind of healing in the world.

A sparkling blue-and-white [globe]... laced with slowly swirling veils of white ... like a small pearl in a thick sea of black mystery.[21]

—*Time*

Geo-Justice is a way of seeing, a metaphor, an operative myth. In that sense, it is like language. Language has many components, but language itself is more than those components; it is a means of expression. Similarly, Geo-Justice has a variety of components. Later in this book, I explore three components: the Global and mystical, the Local and prophetic, and the Psycho-Social. The interaction of these dialectical components moves us to take responsibility for this planet. But Geo-Justice, like language, is more than its components; it is an expression of vision, a process of healing the Earth. With this responsibility, we view Earth and life in a new way.

We have a new perspective, a new Window for the World.
The action that flows from this perspective is the work of Geo-Justice.

Strong forces
Somehow at play
Unleashing
New found hope of integration

Long years of division
Slowly knitting
Into a painful combination
Of love and letting go

Doubts and aspirations
Fly by
In successive bursts
Inviting a new perspective on life

Search for self
Gives place
To a growing cosmic awareness
A quickening grasp of who the me could be

Ocean and mountains beckon
A silent invitation
From the strong and relenting forces
Of the Earth's energetic way

To sit at the feet of the cosmos
Bidden by those majestic forces
That speak the Earth's wisdom—
This untracked route
Somehow I must go

—*Conlon*

Part II

Cosmic crucifixion: dying as a transforming act

Historical perspective

> Someday, after we have mastered the winds, the waves, the tides and gravity, we shall harness for God the energies of love. Then for the second time in the history of the world, man will have discovered fire.[22]
> —*Teilhard de Chardin*

Justice has its roots in the land and the natural order. Wild animals co-exist; they are dependent on each other. Natural justice represents a harmony and balance in which the welfare of the whole is protected. The natural world, at some instinctive level, appears to recognize that broader purpose. Wild herds rarely overgraze the land, exposing it to erosion and degradation, regardless of their numbers.

For humans, justice began in that historical moment when a community recognized its interdependence with the Earth and with each other. Neither the Earth nor the community existed for the benefit of a few—there was no privileged "few," only an inclusive, equality-based culture which complemented a spiritual awakening to the Earth.

Geo-Justice invites us to return to that time when people felt a oneness with the Earth rather than a need to dominate it, to restore a period when befriending, living-with and at-one-ment marked the relationship between people and the planet. Matthew Fox underlines this perspective for our time: "Peace *on* earth cannot happen without peace *with* the earth and peace among all earth creatures."[23]

Moments of harmony

During the medieval period, a moment of harmony and interconnectivity occurred. In this time of cultural ferment, mysticism and prophecy coalesced and erupted into a new experience of the fullness of life. Chartres Cathedral symbolizes this mood of passion, of adventure, of disquietude that ignited an entire culture and filled it with creativity. The writings of the medieval mystics— Francis, Hildegard, Eckhart, Julian, Mechtild, John of the Cross and Aquinas—still excite and stimulate us today.

The Renaissance, similarly, saw a flowering of new beginnings from a spiritual awakening. Again, mysticism and prophecy, sacred and secular, theology and art and science, blended in an outpouring of energy that transformed Western civilization. The Renaissance drew on the past for its roots, and gave them wings in a vision of the future.

More recently, the 1960s, a "mini-middle ages," granted for many of us a glimpse of a culture that dissolved divisions and promoted transformation. This period, though brief, was truly a renaissance moment. From human rights to ecological efforts, new possibilities came bursting forth. The 1960s restored a vision; the decade renewed a hope that profound and authentic change was both possible and expected.

We were convinced then that change could happen, that tomorrow could be different from today. It was a time when we felt that our deepest needs and convictions could be realized, when the rigidity of patriarchal structures would give way to new configurations of inclusion, liberation and hope.

I remember the life and work of Saul David Alinsky, the primary architect of mass-based community organization. Alinsky began a training institute in the late 1960s after seeing his work shut down by the national paranoia of the McCarthy era. A renewed surge of energy came then, and continues in this neo-Alinsky age, whenever we are given the opportunity to respond to our personal and social needs through interest, energy and participation.

I remember visiting African- and Mexican-American families in urban centers like Saginaw, Michigan. In their homes, I found little more than a TV set—and a picture of John XXIII, an old man in Rome whose religion they did not understand or practise, but

37

whose initiative had opened the windows and who was, they knew beyond doubt, their friend. And I remember 1965 in Selma—a benchmark in the decade—an event that attracted civil and religious leaders from all over North America. Selma was a statement for civil rights and a source of renewed hope for oppressed peoples everywhere. Despite what happened three years later—the assassination of King in Memphis on April 8—the road from Alabama to Tennessee, from Selma to Memphis, inspired many people and irreversibly changed history.

Other memories of the 1960s tumble forth: the hippie movement, back to the land, and the Haight-Ashbury phenomenon in San Francisco. Resurrection City in Washington—the tent city of people at the nation's capital gathered to express their solidarity with the poor. More ecclesially, the Urban Training Center for Christian Mission, the Canadian Urban Training Project for Christian Service, and the Catholic Committee on Urban Ministry, led by Msgr. John Egan. All of these provided a new approach to a society and to a church frozen by shock and fear of change.

Perhaps most significantly, it was the time of our first encounter with space. In the lunar landing of July 1969, Neil Armstrong uttered his memorable words: "One small step for man; one giant step for mankind." For the first time, seeing through the eyes of those astronauts, we saw the Earth as one. Our relationship with the earth was changed forever.

It was also a time punctuated by reminders that the era would fall short of our expectations. Publication of the 1968 Vatican document *Humanae Vitae* on family planning and birth control symbolically rang down the curtain on a decade of ecclesial transformation and hoped-for change. A series of assassinations—John F. Kennedy, Martin Luther King Jr., Bobby Kennedy, Malcolm X—demonstrated painfully the entrenched opposition to transformation.

Despite the closure of the windows that had provided inspiration, we moved into the 1970s viewing the future through the eyes of E.F. Schumacher who announced that "small is beautiful." His vision of a viable society was nourished by alternatives that could be incorporated into our culture, rather than repressed by guns, fear and phobia.

The 1980s were a time of increased global awareness. Live Aid made charity worldwide; Michal Gorbachev broke the barriers of the Cold War.

This decade launched us into the 1990s, a time of increased momentum towards oneness with the Earth. More than 200 million people participated in Earth Day, 1990; it was a watershed moment pointing us towards the wonder of a planetary Pentecost, a new experience of oneness in and through the Earth. In the face of the insatiableness of consumerism, this impulse for oneness is revealed by an increased quest for authentic deep mysticism, by a movement away from a fixed and separate world view to an appreciation of ecology, of indigenous peoples' spiritualities, and to health rather than illness.

The characteristics of peace and justice

The years I spent learning from and working with justice-makers reveal some significant characteristics of justice for the Earth. Whatever the project or lifestyle, those engaged in long-term justice activity make connections between their engagement and their spiritual origins. They are transformed and radicalized through their experiences of oppression. As they reflect on their experience and their spiritual journey, they come to see that they can be freed.

Through the work of justice-making, therefore, they become midwives of the new culture, people of Geo-Justice who are themselves being born.

The search for inspiration and support finds continuing expression in many cultural projects of today. The women's and men's movements are working toward gender justice as a framework for living that reflects our deepest aspirations. Their approach is based on ecological and psychic interdependence and balance. Those involved in these movements sense an urgency for a congruence between lifestyle and conviction, between authenticity and strength, confidence and integrity, vision and implementation.

The present moment opens us to the possibilities of new lifestyles, new expressions of leadership, new approaches that are collective in structure, prophetic in stance, and frontier-like in approach. This style of leadership will take us into a new era. The framework of Geo-Justice provides a vehicle for translating in concrete ways the vision bubbling up in the collective unconscious of our culture.

We are being called by the pain of the Earth to be architects of the new era that lies ahead.

Process Reflection

1. Trees are the planetary equivalent of lungs. Form a circle; have each person enter the circle and with an appropriate movement announce, "I speak for (naming a tree from the area)." The group responds, "We hear the voice of the trees."
2. What questions do you find living within you about the nature of Geo-Justice?
3. Try to draw your own mandala (a symbol based on a circle) for a planetary Pentecost. Identify the components of that rebirth; show how they relate to each other.
4. Reflect on your drawing in light of your questions about Geo-Justice. Does your own vision begin to answer your questions?

A planetary earthquake

We are right now in the midst of one of the most traumatic, yet creative, cultural transformations of all human history—a cultural earthquake.[24]

—*Joe Holland*

Albert Nolan writes, "It is by reading the signs of our times that we discover what kind of time we are living in."[25] Justice-making flows out of reading the signs of the times, out of seeing in trends and countertrends what is going on. Until we know that, we cannot decide what needs to happen and what we are willing to take responsibility for changing.

When we fail to read the signs of the times, we are condemned to continue in old patterns. The first step in justice-making is a willingness to break with linear patterns. Justice-making does not deal with an ideal or abstracted world; it starts where we are, right now. The healing of the Earth begins as a response to the cultural moment in which we are living.

At this moment, a growing consciousness envelops the Earth. As our capacity to know the planet as a whole increases, we share a collective consciousness through which the Earth becomes aware of and reflects upon itself. The new understanding of our origins, through art, science and mysticism, has released an enormous energy and interest among a growing number of people pursuing a spirituality of the Earth. The present cultural moment propels us toward a new moment, and a new one beyond that...

Meister Eckhart reminds us that the work of transformation is "Whatever needs to be done."[26] Transformation is not only a response to the demands of the task at hand, it is best accomplished by someone who is open and committed to personal transformation. It is said that true personal transformation happens only on two occasions: when we fall in love or have a "nervous breakdown."

Falling in love can lead to a relentless pursuit of the object of our affection. When we fall in love with a person, we find ways to be with that person. We can also fall in love with a place, an ocean, a cause or an idea. This attraction opens us to beauty. It dissolves the barriers, internal and external, separating us from it. It is truly transformative, for nothing remains the same.

By a "nervous breakdown," I refer to internally trapped energy that, when expressed, is the fuel for personal transformation. We let go of some things that oppressed us, and accept the need to change. Our society is at present going through something very like a "nervous breakdown." We need to let go of some attitudes, suppositions, and systems that were once considered essential. The result will be a cultural earthquake—the breakthrough from breakdown into a new and transformed culture.

A transformation really is taking place in both our consciousness and our culture. Old forms and paradigms are collapsing. We live at the moment of both breakdown and breakthrough. The breakdown invites us to be hospice workers; the breakthrough, to be midwives. By creating a hospice for the culture, a context in which cultural forms can die with dignity, we make it possible for new forms to be born.

There is much evidence of this collapse. A National Mental Health periodical lists a whole range of new resources: programs for victims of crime and domestic violence, material for social workers, a women's guide to safe travel, and resources for single parents. Each of these resources points to a breakdown of the infrastructures of our society—that much is obvious. Less obviously, each of these breakdowns points to new beginnings for particular groups. Thus the signs of breakdown are also the signs of breakthrough.

The emergence of *perestroika* in eastern Europe is a powerful example of this breakdown and breakthrough. It challenges us to bring about *perestroika* in our own land, in our communities, and our own psyches.

This cultural earthquake marks the end of an era. Until now, our value system has operated on "more and better," on compulsion and competition. These values are exemplified in large urban centers. Urban renewal drives out large numbers of people; the result is increased homelessness, with city people becoming urban refugees. When this homelessness is perpetrated more broadly upon the Earth, we have environmental refugees.

A dispassionate survey suggests that we are part of a culture committed to death. Toxic chemicals show up in our food; changes in the ozone layer resulting from industrial activities affect our weather, our health and our crops; our seas and rivers are dying of acid rain and industrial pollution. We are enveloped by poison, consumerism, and militarism.

There are many more indicators of cultural collapse. North America has the highest divorce rate in the world—more than 50% of marriages end in divorce. In Canada, 70% of people remarry, making stepfamilies the most common family form. By the time they reach eighteen, 35% of all children will live with a stepparent. In the U.S., 1300 stepfamilies are formed every day. The North American continent now claims the highest rate of poverty—about 25 percent—for infant and preschool children of any industrialized region. The number of single-parent households, mostly headed by women, has also exploded, along with a huge increase in the number of "latchkey" children coming home to empty houses. Increasingly, day care is not adequate; more and more children will predictably be raised in poverty. Epidemic drug abuse becomes a symptom of our culture whose soul is under siege.

The family becomes merely an economic unit; the values of love receive little support from a consumer-conscious culture.

Schools should be places of learning; they have become places where children are socialized into an increasingly unjust system. Like factories of conformity, schools produce consumers who accept goals that are taken for granted by teachers and society alike. The pressure to compete, to conform, to achieve, robs students of their capacity to pay attention to the deep interior voices that invite them to their unique and irreplaceable contribution to the Earth.

This is both a cultural and a spiritual crisis. But a crisis is also an opportunity for breakthrough. A crisis can launch each of us into the work of personal and social transformation, with social and global consequences.

> [We are] in the midst of a great transformation comparable to the one that confronted medievalism and shook its institutions to the ground... The old ideas and assumptions that made our institutions legitimate are being eroded. They are slipping away in the face of a changing reality, being replaced by different ideas, as yet ill-formed, contradictory, unsettling.[27]
>
> —*George Cabot Lodge*

The signs of transformation

One way to reflect on this cultural collapse is to compare it to major illnesses of our time—**cancer, AIDS** and **heart attacks**.

Physiologically, **cancer** is the runaway reproduction of cells in a biological organism. In Western civilization, we have the runaway technology of a post-industrial age.

This unbounded growth pattern has produced overpopulated cities stifling on their own garbage all over the world. Walk the streets of New York some evening, and you can see this cancer for yourself. The average North American uses 600 pounds of paper per year, compared to 15 pounds per person in developing countries; our forests are being consumed at the rate of more than a football field per second.

Around the world, militarism and its inevitable partner, tyranny, proliferate out of control in country after country. Pollution spews smoke and dust, acids and toxins, and "greenhouse gases" to circulate globally through the atmosphere, like leukemia in the bloodstream. From the dawn of the industrial revolution, smoke stacks have disgorged noxious gases into the atmosphere. Factories dump wastes into rivers and streams; automobiles gobble irreplaceable fossil fuels. In the name of progress, forests have been denuded, lakes poisoned, and underground aquifers pumped dry. Earth's occupants hover on the threshold of ecocide and genocide. Yes, the Earth has cancer.

AIDS—Acquired Immune Deficiency Syndrome—sends shockwaves of fear among us. AIDS is a breakdown in the immune system of the human body. At present, AIDS has no cure. It promises certain death.

The Earth also has AIDS. Her species are dying, her water is poisoned and her topsoil destroyed; she is losing her capacity to regenerate and heal.

Humans get **heart attacks** when their arteries are blocked by the fatty deposits resulting from over-rich living and stress. The arteries in our bodies correspond to the dammed waterways of our streams and rivers, and the daily traffic jams of highways and airports. Ivan Illich says that it is difficult to explain to people from a primitive culture why a machine designed to go 120 mph travels at no more than 15 mph in a twice-daily "traffic jam." Automotive gridlock is a sign of our "cultural cholesterol." In 1975, *Time* magazine estimated that 40 percent of urban roads were congested. Today, it is more like 75 percent. Some commuters virtually live on the freeways.

Our transportation arteries seem desperately in need of a bypass operation! But simply building more highways will not cure the illness.

Bodily illnesses require a change of lifestyle. So do cultural and ecological illnesses. If the healing of bodily ills is connected to a person's spiritual health, the healing of a culture depends on a spiritual awakening. As we explore and begin to understand our bodies, our culture, and our world, we will find there the wisdom to guide us toward our future.

Opportunity for transformation

The cultural earthquake our civilization is experiencing makes many of us aware of an accompanying personal crisis. We have a sense of growing disparity between our life and work and the divine summons to our unique lifestyle, our true vocation. We are dissatisfied. We sense something greater to give birth to, some work or call to which we still must respond.

This increasing dis-ease becomes a life crisis. As long as we resist or block the cosmic truth of our lives, the crisis intensifies. This condition, for me, is a kind of "psychic colitis." When disruptive health patterns constrict its proper function, the colon rebels. In the same way, when we constrict the flow of divine energy in our lives, our very beings rebel. Seeing crisis as an opportunity for breakthrough will enable us to become more open to our true destiny. We will experience life as more pleasurable, profound, meaningful, and compassionate.

I frequently meet people who report that a crisis in their lives became an opportunity that propelled them into new life. Usually, they were blocking some truth about themselves. Through continual resistance, the crisis intensified. Just as a boil swells and breaks, so the crisis culminated—in a broken relationship, loss of a job, illness, or chemical dependency. But only through that crisis did they discover a truer direction for their lives.

I heard an AIDS patient say, "Avoid the virus, but expose yourself to AIDS." Hospice workers often ask their patients, "How has cancer blessed your life?" I have met people recovering from heart attacks who told me that the illness had worked a new beginning in their lives. David Crombie, the former mayor of Toronto, Canada, once quipped: "You'd go broke selling heart attacks door to door—but it was the best thing that ever happened to me!"

From apparent tragedy emerges the beginning of new life. The earthquake that surrounds us is a precondition for the unfolding planetary Pentecost.

Our challenge as workers in Geo-Justice is to see how the AIDS, cancer and heart attacks of the Earth are signs of resurrection and not just of death. Theologically, they are an intense and critical enactment of the Paschal mystery in our midst. A friend told me that a small and simple sign had reduced roadside garbage in Texas by almost 60 percent. The sign merely reminded drivers, "Don't Mess with Texas." It's a sign of inspiration and of hope.

We will only achieve a new understanding by immersing

ourselves in these crises of the world, not by escaping from them. Geo-Justice calls us to immerse ourselves in the fabric of life. History teaches us that engagement in life is a prerequisite for cultural transformation.

A time of transition

The mid-life transition offers another analogy through which to see society. Research suggests that the leaders of the cultural revolutions of the past have usually been people going through their own mid-life transition. The ferment in their lives shattered their complacency, and they saw both themselves and society in a different light.

The dynamics of breakdown and breakthrough in a society reflect the individual experience of transition. Change, for a society or an individual, begins with a sense of disquiet, a recognition that all is not as it should be, and that events are moving us forward involuntarily. Neither an individual nor a culture can stay stuck in personal or social malaise.

As a culture, we stand poised at that awesome moment of transition, that moment of letting go of the past and awaiting something new to emerge. Like acrobats on a trapeze, we have to let go of one rope before we can grab for the next. We don't know what will come. But we are sure something will come forth from the ambiguity of this moment. Such an event could be called the *perestroika* of our cultural soul.

As midwives for a new ecological era and hospice workers for a culture about to die, we need to address two important questions:
• What needs to be born?
• What needs to die?

Within the context of the Paschal mystery (the dynamics of death and Resurrection) the connection between what needs to be born and what needs to die is dialectical. Dying is a transformative act which is recycled into new life.

A litany for transformation

One possible response to these questions of birth and death is to compose a litany. What connections can we make between the poor of the Earth and the poor Earth? Between what is, and what can be? In the example that follows, I first offer what needs to be born (the Resurrection component); then I can see what needs to die (the cross dimension) before the Resurrection can happen. I have arranged these antiphonally, to emphasize the possibilities of break-through embodied in this cultural moment.

Trust needs to be born,
Security needs to die;
Liberation needs to be born,
Oppression needs to die;
Celebration needs to be born,
Boredom needs to die;
Connectedness needs to be born,
Alienation needs to die;
Global awareness needs to be born,
Nation-state-ism needs to die;
Creativity and courage need to be born,
Fear of death needs to die;
The right brain needs to be born,
The left brain needs to be happy about it;
Feminism needs to be born,
Patriarchy needs to die;
Soul-making needs to be born,
Individualism needs to die;
Recovery needs to be born,
Addiction needs to die;
Playing together needs to be born,
Competing needs to die;
The Ecological Age needs to be born,
Environmental genocide needs to die;
Reverence for all life needs to be born,
Domination and objectification need to die;
Doing-with needs to be born,
Doing-for needs to die;
Be-attitude needs to be born,
Have-attitude needs to die;
Hope needs to be born,
Despair needs to die;
Creative silence needs to be born,

Empty noise needs to die;
Awareness needs to be born,
Insensitivity needs to die;
Circles need to be born,
Hierarchies need to die;
Dialectic needs to be born,
Dualism needs to die;
Laughter and tears need to be born,
Sadness and sentimentality need to die;
A new order of Geo-Justice needs to be born,
The old order needs to die.

You can easily create your own litany, of actions and concerns that matter to you. We must recycle more, procreate less, turn lights off, use mass transit—in short, do a thousand things differently.

We need to identify these actions, these changes, to focus our efforts. As humankind enters the last decade of the 20th century, we are at a crucial point. The actions of those now living will determine the future and possibly the very survival of the planet.

Signposts for Geo-Justice

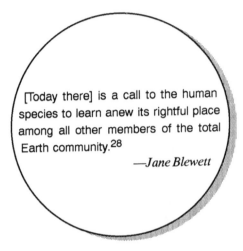

[Today there] is a call to the human species to learn anew its rightful place among all other members of the total Earth community.[28]

—*Jane Blewett*

Three signposts can help us discover the nature of our participation in the work of Geo-Justice. These three are **planet, place,** and **path**. They can perhaps be best recognized in three questions.

- "What are my roots?" (my relationship to the **planet**)
- "What is my work in Geo-Justice?" (my **place**)
- "Who am I?" (my **path**)

Planet, place and path—these three signposts point each of us toward our particular participation in Geo-Justice. In seeking answers to the questions that represent planet, place, and path, we recognize that we ourselves are a microcosm of the cosmos we attempt to nurture. In this way we view the psyche, and the whole human organism, within the context of the culture and the universe. We have a direction; we are going somewhere; we are an arrow toward the future. Focusing on planet, place and path helps us to challenge our present perceptions, collapse stereotypes of self, and move beyond the present toward the future.

People everywhere are searching for a response to these questions. One person I think of is a systems analyst on the West Coast; another is a taxi driver in New England; a third is a journalist from

Europe. In each case, their personal experiences of life transitions mirror the larger transitions taking place in society. In a sense, they are archetypes of those who are exploring new approaches to purpose and contribution, to origin and destiny. They know that they will find no full or final answers to their questions. But they celebrate revelatory moments, palpable instants of contact with the divine in events both common and profound.

As Thomas Merton said: "If I never become what I am meant to be, but always remain what I am not, I shall spend eternity contradicting myself by being at once something and nothing..."[29]

For all of these people, a profound sense of **homecoming** (planet), **woundedness** (place), and **spirituality** (path), identify their motivation.

> The world cannot be discovered by a journey of miles, no matter how long, but only by a spiritual journey, a journey of one inch, very arduous and humbling and joyful, by which we arrive at the ground at our feet, and learn to be at home.[30]
>
> —*Wendell Berry*

Homecoming

This planet is our home. We have no other home. But vast numbers of people have no sense of Earth as their home. Lacking roots, they have no sense of homecoming.

Years ago, while I was a student at the Canadian Urban Training Project, I wrote about the rootlessness of single displaced men who came to the Fred Victor Mission in Toronto's inner city.

The Monks of Skid Row
A strange breed of monks, these 12,000 derelicts of life,
These lovable genial isolated human beings
They live with a past not to be forgotten,

A present built out of isolation,
And a future that promises and hopes for nothing.
These monks of the inner city are more alone
Than the strictest contemplative...
And often more redeemed
As they traffic in their currency of cigarettes,
Where to get beer, a bed, a meal, a job and sometimes money,
They are selfless and concerned.
These islands of humanity boasting of a day's work
And regretting a wasted life—
They trust NO ONE as they walk
Their silent world of pain and fear,
This order of the street, men without futures, without rights—
Poor, pushed, passed by and possessed
By those who provide beds and food,
Keeping them on one aimless treadmill of life.
They live without solutions,
With no one listening to what they say,
No one asking them to talk,
Inviting them to spill, to drain
The poison from their lives,
A poison that festers in nightmares, alcohol,
Fear of work, passive acceptance of mistreatment,
unexpressed anger and fear.

Working with transients, and wandering the streets myself on an urban "plunge," I shared their experience of homelessness. I realized for the first time how homelessness has turned city dwellers into urban refugees, people who live in "cardboard condos." Unlike the rest of us, they have no "home" to come home to.

We all need a home. Our homecoming, in that sense, is about returning to our origins, to celebrate our roots. Not just to come home to the farms where our ancestors once lived, but to come home to the universe, to the Earth, to our culture, our traditions, and ourselves—and to accept all of this as home.

Homecoming celebrates the interconnectedness of all reality. It is a spirituality of "Aha!"—a sometimes startled recognition of who we are, and where we have come from. We belong. We feel a comfortable congruence of our life with the life of the planet, an experience of peace that provides the security to free us from clinging to past practices.

Homecoming recognizes that we came of the Earth, are of the Earth, and will return to the Earth. We reclaim our origins, our starting point. And each time we go back to that starting point, we begin again. So our work in Geo-Justice is always new, always as Berry wrote, "a spiritual journey... by which... we learn to be at home."

> To recognize the sufferings of our time in our own heart and make that recognition the starting point of service to enter into a dislocated world...will not be perceived as authentic unless it comes from a heart wounded by the suffering about which it speaks.[31]
> —Adapted from Henri Nouwen

Woundedness

Henri Nouwen's concept of the "wounded healer" shows us the wisdom of place. Our wounds are not just our own—they are also the wounds of the cosmos. When we explore our pain, we discover where our strength and our freedom are, and where justice lies. When our personal pain becomes cosmic pain, when cosmic pain becomes our personal pain, we are energized to heal the Earth.

Our current cultural and ecological crises show us the futility of resolving our personal problems at the expense of others or of the environment. Similarly, we will accomplish nothing if we try to heal the wounds of the Earth by inflicting ever-more wounds upon ourselves. The most appropriate energy for our work is that which brings healing to **both** ourselves and society.

Often people discover, when they examine their lives, that what they feel most passionate about reflects their pain. They recognize that, as Nouwen wrote, their heart is "wounded by the suffering about which it speaks."

Our woundedness indicates our capacity for compassion in a wounded world. Our pain and the pain of the planet are catalysts to work toward oneness in the universe. In the work of Geo-Justice, we "atone" for the past—that is, we make ourselves "at one" with the cosmos. Our vulnerability to the pain of the Earth, like a psychic compass, guides our destiny. Our woundedness reveals our place on the planet; we find our place as we seek to heal the wounds of the Earth.

If creating a new culture for the ecological age is the next phase of our experience, creating an integral spirituality may well be the next phase of the Christian tradition.[32]
—*Adapted from Thomas Berry*

Spirituality

Spirituality moves us beyond concerns of career and ambition to a continuing process of change and completion. Spirituality is an awakening to the depths of who we are, an unfolding of our own story. It generates an understanding of ourselves and the Earth. It affirms connections between the universe and the culture. We engage fully in the here and now, without regretting the past or fearing the future; the experiences of our lives are the context in which we discover our path to our place on the planet.

We can only know what we're supposed to be by awakening to what we already are in the depths of our own souls. Brian Swimme says of that awakening: "If we pursue these paths, our lives—even should they become filled with suffering and hardship—are filled as well with the quality of effortlessness."[33]

Spirituality speaks of our souls. Therefore it speaks deeply to our experience. An integral spirituality will not invite us to withdraw. Rather, it invites us into life as an unlimited possibility. It offers hope, opportunity, possibility and future.

For the new era of global interdependence, we need a mature spirituality that reverences creation for its own sake, a spirituality that understands our perception of creation through the senses as an experience of the divine. We need to be able to deal with social structures as well as personal attitudes, with multinational corporations as well as family life. For we are dealing here with our whole civilization, our whole planet.

Thomas Berry writes, "Presently we are returning to the primordial community of the universe, the Earth, and all living beings...each has its special symbolism. The excitement of life is in the numinous experience wherein we are given to each other in that larger celebration of existence... The universe, by definition, is a single gorgeous celebratory event."[34]

This is a transformative path. Its wisdom shows us how to live in resonance with the Earth. Teilhard de Chardin summarized this approach: "I became aware that I was losing contact with myself. At each step of the descent a new person was disclosed within me of whose name I was no longer sure and who no longer obeyed me. And when I had to stop my exploration because the path faded beneath my steps, I found a bottomless abyss at my feet, and out of it comes—arising I know not from where—the current which I dare to call my life."[35]

In a time of cultural dislocation and personal uncertainty, the psyche and soul are no longer storehouses of what has gone before, but arrows flying fearlessly into the future.

Process Reflection:

1. How do we go about building new structures, new forms and ways of doing things, new centers of energy for a cultural genesis in our day? How do we change things without repeating the tyrannies of our present culture, even if it is for a different cause? Where do we start?

2. How do we build mediating institutions between the powerful structures of greed that dominate our lives, and

the gentler forms designed for nurture that show up here and there? How, in fact, do we nurture the structures that nurture?

3. How can we bring about a consciousness of Geo-Justice, an awareness of a planetary Pentecost, an awakening to living out the mysticism and prophecy that emerges from the deepest part of people and the planet?

4. What do you think needs to be born and what needs to die?

Part III

Making
our Easter
with the Earth

The components of Geo-Justice

Making our Easter with the Earth

The moments of resurrection and liberation in Geo-Justice are developed through three components: global, local, and psycho-social. They are like identifiable parts of the "stew" that is Geo-Justice. They interact with and influence each other.

For example, when rubber workers in Brazil became involved in saving the Amazon rain forests, their initial motivation was their own livelihood. Subsequently, they came to see themselves involved in the ecological agenda of the planet. Their local involvement, as well as having global implications, also profoundly affected their own psyches.

When change occurs in one component, it affects the others. In this dynamic system, components overlap: the global with the local, the local with the psycho-social, the innermost mystical experience with the prophetic. Looking at any one component is like using a zoom lens on a camera—we focus on one element of the whole picture, always remembering that it remains part of a larger unity. So as we focus on one component of Geo-Justice, we need to keep in mind its interconnection with other components. The global, local, and psycho-social intersect and interact; a change in any one has implications for the whole system. Our psyches affect, and are affected by, the local and global communities, and all three function within the processes of the cosmos and the Earth.

As we explore these components of Geo-Justice, we open ourselves to resurrection moments, when we make our Easter with the Earth.

As animators of Geo-Justice, each of us joins in an adventure that began 15 billion years ago. Our quest finds expression in the three principles of the universe: communion, differentiation, and interiority. These three principles find their cultural expression in Geo-Justice through a holistic synthesis of the global, local, and psycho-social components.

Taken together, these three components bring us to a cultural moment of Resurrection, in which our adventure celebrates communion with the natural world. We see everything attached to everything else, to all species and all creation. The global component of Geo-Justice expresses a longing for oneness with the Earth as a whole, and for prophetic action from a global perspective.

The adventure acknowledges—and is—the expression of diversity. That everything is unique is reflected in all aspects of the universe. We celebrate that diversity in recognizing the uniqueness of each local region of the Earth, and the particular gifts, creativity, and destinies of each member of creation.

The compassionate culmination of our adventurous quest for Geo-Justice is guided by listening to our own inner voice, and by hearing the voices of the natural world. Reflection on our interior life, and exploration of its application to our culture and to creation, is found in the psycho-social component of Geo-Justice.

The global component

To become at the same time, and by the same act, one with all, through release from all multiplicity or material gravity: there you have, deeper than any ambition for pleasure, for wealth or power, the essential dream of the human soul.[36]

—*Teilhard de Chardin*

A vehicle for healing

Our experiences of being at one with the Earth remind us that how we treat the Earth is how we treat ourselves.

In our culture, healing usually concentrates on the individual, sometimes at the expense of society. Thus individuals demand their "rights," regardless of the impact of those rights on others. Or healing may attempt to improve the health of a larger body—a nation, a group of nations, the world community—at the expense of individual members of that larger body. That has been our characteristic treatment of our native peoples. Conventional concepts of healing thus are usually exclusive, separate, and dualistic.

Geo-Justice, by contrast, is inclusive and dialectical. It respects both the individual and the group. Because its foundational precept is the sense of oneness with the Earth, it provides a perspective that respects diversity and differences among global communities and cultures. With Geo-Justice, awareness moves from individual rights or national sovereignty toward a planetary perspective. It is ecologically conscious and deeply ecumenical. Instead of "me," or "my family," or "my country," we start to think of a world community.

Nourished by mysticism—an experience of oneness—this community finds expression in political and economic organizations that serve a new global civilization. Instead of defending ourselves by separating from others, we work toward a world order that transcends national differences.

Mysticism refers to those experiences, when, through a shift in consciousness, we feel at one with the Earth. The experience of oneness does not blur the complexity and diversity of the Earth community; it enables us to feel united to the Earth as a whole and to know our place within it. The experience of mysticism has been described as an experience of giving birth and remaining mindful. Meister Eckhart speaks of this when he says, "It is that which flows out, yet remains within."[37]

Mysticism is about awe, beauty, and wonder. It is about our experience of ultimate reality. Focused on the Earth, mysticism expands our perspective. It enables us to dissolve differences, to find a common language and common images for a common work, focused on the healing and renewal of the planet. *Global* mysticism combines the macro and micro in a single experience: consciousness of ourselves, *and* a new-found consciousness of the entire planet. We see the Earth as what Pope Pius XII's encyclical called *Mystici Corporis*, the mystical body.

Mystical awareness is the deepest anchor for global solidarity.[38]
—*David Steindl-Rast*

As the planetary crisis intensifies, global mysticism becomes a vehicle for healing the devastation that surrounds us. Through our oneness with the Earth, we begin to see the structural implications of global interdependence. Instead of merely being mechanics for national systems, we become architects of international and transcultural systems. As we begin to understand in a new way our relationship to the Earth, our perspective on unity gives birth to global structures.

We are global citizens reflecting on ourselves and on the world. We examine political, cultural and economic dimensions to transform them. We are, in a sense, doctors rather than diagnosticians. At the same time, we are ourselves in need of healing.

The power of mysticism

The late Marshall McLuhan called our planet a "Global Village." McLuhan referred primarily to the communications technology that makes information exchange possible anywhere on the planet. But he also implied the mystical consciousness that enables us to recognize ourselves as part of the whole. Our consciousness can envelop the Earth. This awareness of the Earth as a whole is analogous to seeing "global weather patterns." When we watch cloud patterns swirling over the Earth in a satellite image, we know that what affects us also affects others considerable distances away.

This global consciousness shifts our approach to the Earth from domination to equity. Thomas Berry writes in the *Riverdale Papers*, "Our spirituality is Earth derived—the thoughts and emotions, the social forms and rituals of the human community are as much Earth as is the soil and the rocks and the trees and the flowers."[39]

This awareness of our oneness with the Earth promotes the kind of consciousness required for Geo-Justice. Berry goes so far as to propose that we are, in fact, through our intellect and our ability to reflect, a unique component of the Earth, "that aspect through which the universe reflects upon itself." As humans we are "the psyche of the universe" or "the consciousness of the world." Our role as the consciousness of the Earth creates a climate for global questioning and reflection.

There are, basically, two kinds of analysis—"macro" and "micro." The term "micro" is more familiar to most of us. We use it in "microscope," for example, or "microphone." It simply means "small." Micro-analysis puts things under a microscope—we attempt to understand them by examining, in great detail, some minute component of the whole.

"Macro"-analysis refers to a study of the forces at play on a larger scale. Weather patterns make a good example again. Micro-analysis might study the effect of Lake Michigan on winter temperatures in Chicago; macro-analysis would try to understand that same Chicago winter weather by integrating the effects of ozone layer depletion, the position and strength of the jet stream, and ocean currents in the South Pacific.

Many groups today deal with justice issues from a local perspective; many others engage in their work from a global perspective. What seems frequently missing is an understanding of the micro/macro interrelationship—everything is related to everything else. Any part potentially contains within itself the whole; the whole affects every part.

We need a global perspective on problems and issues. That perspective needs to be energized by a mystical consciousness. Our present experience of cultural collapse is accompanied by a sense of increased complexity, a sense that everything is blurred and unclear. The mystical component for justice-making underlines the need for an enhanced awareness of planetary interdependence. This interdependence affects all life forms, from microbes to tropical forests to political and economic systems. This awareness complements and supports major shifts in our world view, and reinforces the image of the Earth as sacred.

I believe that this kind of global mysticism is emerging. Projects for justice and peace increasingly adopt a world perspective. Human rights organizations cut across national boundaries to encourage global systems of justice. Moment by moment, the focus on information and support on a planetary scale increases. This direction is a concrete basis for hope. It taps into the transformation needed at all levels of existence.

The age of nations is past. The task before us now, if we would not perish, is to build the earth.[40]

—*Teilhard de Chardin*

63

Practical applications

Standing on the threshold of the future, we become aware of the challenge of discovering new solutions, new approaches, new frameworks of action, and new strategies. If we genuinely look to Geo-Justice, we will seek those practices that are hope-filled, and that offer practical alternatives.

Currently, we can observe the disintegration of reactionary trends in governments and churches. We see a collapse of established leadership, and at the same time an increased willingness to trust others. The age of political and economic dogmatism is coming to an end.

We search for an analysis and approach that affirms the Earth, as a whole, as the only reliable context for life and for the resolution of life's problems. No longer is it appropriate to refer to the nations of the First, Second and Third worlds. Resolution, rather, resides within acknowledgment of global interdependence. We search for strategies and solutions within a global context.

Emphatically, we need to support the efforts of justice-makers who approach their efforts from the global context. We must develop a global context of information, support and common action as a vehicle to support the efforts of each project and collectively enhance the work of world justice. Global networks increase our capacity to encourage fuller participation in healing the planet. Two projects of this kind are "The Campaign for the Earth," with a cooperative strategy for individuals and groups, and "Earth Net," a global telecommunications network designed to support the campaign for the Earth. No single project is sufficient by itself; together, all such projects contribute to that mystical awareness of the whole Earth of which we are a unique and special part.

As a part of the whole, we cannot place our trust in practices that expect the action to come from *others*.

We need to be cautious about any analysis that is only either "micro" or "macro." When we explore the dynamic interaction of the connected components of the planet, we must avoid falling into a "parts mentality" that isolates one aspect of our concerns from all the other aspects.

Many of my own experiences in the past have not included the global perspective. To overlook the broader focus can leave us open to being co-opted by the special interests of multinational forces and thus neutralized. Global Education Associates and others have pointed out that the straight-jacket of nation-state-ism is not a viable context from which to solve global problems. They suggest that we need a more mature spirituality to respond to the challenge of this new era of global interdependence. Instead of strengthening individual nations, we need to build structures for planetary peace. We need nothing less than a new world order. Such an order will respond compassionately to the brokenness of peoples, the woundedness of nations, and the suffering of the Earth.

The earth is the ground of the new world order; a biocracy, that is truly democratic, where every species has a voice; a constellation of relationships that honors memories, story, spirit, and surprise. The experience of oneness with all of life reminds us that peace is possible.

Berry addresses the focus of this component: "We cannot discover ourselves without first discovering the universe, the Earth, and the imperatives of our own being. Each of these has a creative power and a vision far beyond any rational thought or cultural creation of which we are capable. Nor should we think of these as isolated from our own individual being or from the human community. We have no existence except within the Earth and within the universe."[41]

Justice becomes no longer a moral obligation, but rather a deep communion with all that is, and with the planet itself.

When I see how a mystical consciousness can heal and can energize a global analysis and action, I know that it must be a major component of Geo-Justice.

Process Reflection

1. Set up a mood that invites mysticism: slides, music, related readings from the mystics; take time for silence and meditation. Bring something of the earth, and something that expresses a growing worldwide unity.
2. In groups of four or five (or, if no group is available, as an individual) reflect on your own mystical experiences, those transcendent moments when you were aware of being a part of something much larger than yourself.

3. For groups, present a panel, discussing the significance of the global moments of our lives; for individuals, reflect on how mystical experiences broaden your awareness to a truly global perspective.
4. In plenary, encourage responses to presentations and sharing of personal moments of unity with the cosmos.
5. Summarize the common themes emerging from discussion and responses.
6. Closing rituals: gather in a circle to symbolize a mandala for healing the Earth.

The local component

Life is an adventure of passion, risk, danger, laughter, beauty, love, a burning curiosity to go with the action to see what it is all about, to search for a pattern of meaning, to burn one's bridges because you're never going to go back anyway...[42]

—*Saul Alinsky*

A context for action

A true *global* perspective will always energize *local* as well as global strategies for action. It helps us to find imaginative ways to be prophetic in the concrete context of our lives. Instead of feeling helpless or overwhelmed, we begin to apply our aspirations within our own experience.

The global perspective I discussed in the previous section finds its concrete expression in the local bioregion—the geographic and social area in which we live. Here spirituality and action merge.

In the local component of Geo-Justice, social and ecological concerns converge. Restoration of the Earth occurs first on the bioregional level, as we awaken to our roots both in nature and in culture. The opposite—environmental oppression—occurs when minority communities are chosen as toxic dumpsites, when suburbs spread unchecked over farmland, or when forestry logs old-growth forests. All emphasize one concern over another. Geo-Justice brings a synthesis of social and economic concerns into ecological justice. We become present to the natural world in a respectful and non-evasive way, while at the same time seeing our oneness with nature as an indication of right relationships within society and with the planet.

The concrete action that identifies the local component of Geo-Justice is focused and energized by a deep mystical spirituality. The bioregion is the place to respond to the invitation, "Bloom where you are planted." Poet Gary Snyder writes, "Bioregionalism is a fancy form for staying put and learning what is going on."[43]

Listening and recognition

The Local component of Geo-Justice starts with *listening* and *recognition*. Listening is the most profound act of recognition we can extend to another. To act with integrity, we must "learn what is going on." As Paulo Freire is fond of saying, we must "become wet with the soul of the people." Then—and only then—can we act prophetically. As fields are planted and plowed to be planted again, so listening and recognizing continuously calls forth the new from the old, birth from death, and development from decline.

This approach creates solidarity and common ground—the capacity to act from within our deepest aspirations. We begin to see "the world itself as a living being, made up of dynamic aspects," as Starhawk writes, where "all things have inherent value [and are] interrelated in patterns."[44]

Thus, this component of Geo-Justice grounds us in the everyday fabric of our existence. We learn to listen; we recognize our place in the cosmic scheme of things. Our efforts are punctuated by epiphanies—that is, our work becomes a manifestation of the divine. Though it is expressed in concrete action, the Local component acknowledges mystery, because it simultaneously roots us in the Earth and enhances an appreciation of our place as sacred space.

Richard Harmon, staff person with the Brooklyn Ecumenical Cooperatives, works from this perspective. He illustrates this approach with a story about a renovated housing project. When it was opened, some three hundred people gathered to place their hands on the project, to claim their homes as sacred space. That action was both local and prophetic; in it, both concrete fact and deep mystery were acknowledged.

The Local approach weaves together a tapestry of action and numinous mystery. Each thread affects the whole tapestry; each part, each action, has its own integrity. It is alive; each action can continue to influence events. And it is mysterious, for it engages us at a very deep level.

As we develop the mystical consciousness and global analysis dimensions of Geo-Justice, we discover that the process of justice-making for the whole Earth cries out for a local perspective. Albert Nolan, in *God In South Africa*, writes, "The paradigm that shapes every prophetic movement, no matter what its context, is simply this—the time has come, the day is near."[45] That urgency, that imperative to do *something*, certainly characterizes our time.

Concrete action is nourished by an awareness of global forces. Without an understanding of the macro level, local efforts—like the preservation of local jobs at the expense of environmental degradation—can become self-defeating. Inversion of power patterns can become a substitute for conversion.

W. H. Auden once uttered the aphorism, "Those who don't know history tend to repeat it." By developing a global/local imagination, we can hold in dynamic tension the part and the whole, the micro and the macro, the prophetic and the mystical, the local and the global, the past and the future. We examine the movements of the past to nourish our imaginations and to critique present actions. The Agrarian Protest of the last century, the Labor Struggle of the 1920s, the Black Power Movement of the 1950s and '60s, the work of Community Organization from the '60s to today—all give us insights into present justice work. They also give us courage for the future. A recollection of the Civil Rights Movement reveals the amount of energy generated for church and society by the prophetic work of Martin Luther King, Jr. In the local component, history is an important teacher.

Experience and history teach us that the justice-makers have always been a minority. Yet that minority provides compassion, hope, and inspiration for many. The Canadian Conference of Catholic Bishops, in their 1976 Labor Day message, "From Words to Action," called those engaged in action for justice a "significant minority." Our hope for Geo-Justice is to broaden that "significant minority." We need more people engaged in long-term efforts to liberate the structures and emotions that hold us back.

This process is not evaluated by "winning and losing." We can view it only from a perspective that sees the struggle itself as victory, and success as a commitment to a different world view. The only failure is the failure to be hopeful, to be involved, and to learn from our experiences.

In this process, we will move from self-interest to social interest, and beyond. For our social interests themselves are connected to the global community, and the global human community to the Earth itself. Feminist author Virginia Griffin has written: "I know I am made from the earth."[46]

The first act of justice-making

If I am right that our culture does have a growing sense of urgency—if, as Albert Nolan writes, "the time has come, the day is near"—then Geo-Justice is a timely vision. It comes into being, not as the perception of a few isolated individuals, but as an expression of collective consciousness. It flows out of mysticism, prophecy, and personal transformation. It provides fresh energy to justice-makers, who no longer perceive themselves as marginalized minorities but as participants in a new world community.

Igniting the justice imagination involves creating a narrative context where the drama of people's lives can unfold. Hope comes alive through new images, new myths that emerge from the people's lived experiences. From this approach to creativity comes the focused energy necessary to transform a culture. Only then can we empower the building of civil and economic alternatives for the future.

The process of organizing for justice reveals how deeply it is connected to the dynamics of spiritual and personal transformation. When I studied community organization at the Industrial Areas Foundation: Saul Alinsky Training Institute, I found four distinct phases in the organizational process.

The preliminary or **Pre-Organizing Phase** catches the moment of increased hope, when possibility overcomes resignation and passive acceptance. In a community, this moment is usually accompanied by an experience of discovery, delight and awe.

Next comes the **Dis-Organizing Phase,** the dismantling and letting go of structures that are not on the side of people and that are, in fact, instruments of oppression rather than liberation.

The third **Organizing Phase** brings into existence new forms and structures to respond to the needs and interests of those people who are not yet represented by existing structures. This is a breakthrough phase. All kinds of creativity bursts forth.

Finally, the **Re-Organizing Phase** involves applying these new and already developed structures to the interests of the people, to transform both society and themselves.

It is important to recognize that as instruments of transformation we are involved in transformation ourselves. We too go through all four of these phases. So we move from apathy to hope, from hope to letting go, from letting go to creativity, and finally to applying the energy of creativity in ways that change us and our societal relationships.

Out of my experience with the Industrial Areas Foundation: Saul Alinsky Institute, I believe that the Local component of Geo-Justice depends on imagination and courage. It is not learned in a classroom, or from a book. Rather, it is written in people's lives. It is conceived out of struggle. We learn it by getting up each morning and putting ourselves on the line against the forces that would hold us back. It is grasped in the pain of constant effort, of moving people from where they are to where they want to be.

Storytelling—a starting point

I suggest that the starting point for applying the local component is the narrative approach of storytelling. By telling our own stories, and by reflecting imaginatively on our lives, our ancestral roots, our relationship to the land, we will discover elements that have previously gone unnoticed. We may discover powerful memories of nurture in our childhood, or of selflessness in parenthood. By listening to others' stories, and by telling our own stories, we can recognize approaches that will motivate our efforts, and that will promote prophetic actions that reveal divine presence.

Storytelling, in this perspective, is the most radical approach to organizing that is available to us. I remember a student telling her story; in the telling, she discovered her grandmother's commitment to justice in a textile union. I urge you to provide this opportunity for the individuals and groups with whom you work.

The local component, grounded in listening and recognition, is

71

energized by storytelling. Overall, it flows from a new understanding of our relationship to the Earth. We listen to and recognize our own stories; we listen to and recognize the Earth's story. Through storytelling, we strive to end what Madonna Kolbenschlag called "the dualism between planner and planned, organization and environment, corporation and society, culture and nature."[47]

Local and prophetic belong together with the mystical. The **prophetic** element demands engagement; one cannot be prophetic in the abstract. The **local** element demands engagement here and now, in our own context. The **mystical** opens our hearts to the experience of unity.

The following statements about a spirituality of the Earth come from the reflections of a class:

- A way of compassion; a way of caring for all beings/all things; of midwifing a new age of the Spirit in union with our brothers and sisters (and our planet).
- The creative process that empowers people to recognize and find the means to fulfill their needs, to make their dreams come true.
- Grassroots action is a channel of energy for the Earth.
- The struggle to recognize always the grass roots.
- Real democracy which springs from total awareness.
- A structured improvisational dance which demands my full attention and presence to keep up with its moment-by-moment changes.
- Quilting a web of recognition—a divine epiphany of joy.

My own training as a community organizer and my work as an educator with justice-makers has convinced me that although research, analysis and self-knowledge are crucial, action is irreplaceable. Without the local component, Geo-Justice could lack immediate action. Action, seasoned by self-knowledge and empowered by a global perspective, brings authenticity and energy to the task. This conviction first prompted me to include the Local component in the Geo-Justice mandala.

Saul David Alinsky, the architect of community organizing, articulated his passion for this component in an interview shortly before his death. Referring to people in our culture, he said:

They're oppressed by taxation and inflation, poisoned by pollution, terrorized by urban crime, frightened by the new youth culture, baffled by the computerized world around them. They've worked all their lives to get their own little house in the suburbs, their color TV, their two cars, and now the good life seems to have turned to ashes in their mouths... Their society seems to be crumbling, and they see themselves as no more than small failures within a larger failure. All their values seem to have deserted them, leaving them rudderless in a sea of social chaos... We'll not only give them a cause, we'll make life exciting for them again—life instead of existence.[48]

Process Reflection

1. Begin by spending five minutes doing the following:
   a) Tell another person the most deeply felt need in your heart; listen to the other person's deeply felt need. Reflect on the sacred moments emerging from this conversation. What dream of how your life could be emerges from your imagination?
   b) Discuss what a prophet is. Prepare statements that could be accompanied by appropriate music.
   c) Share a vision of your bioregional context, and of what the future could be.
2. Pass a globe around while envisioning a local task to be done.
3. Envision a global task from a Local perspective. Then relate to that task in one of these ways:
   a) Pass out blank puzzle pieces of paper to each person; have each person draw a symbol on that paper, name the Local action, and list people who are prophets for them. When participants are ready, have them put the puzzle together.
   b) Or, pass out packages with props for dramatizing local action.
4. In small groups, think back three or more generations and tell each other about your ancestors' relationship to the land.
5. Reflect in the full group on reactions to the assembled puzzle or dramatic actions with all of its symbols and names; reflect on your particular approach to the local component.

73

6. Envision your local response through clay or another art form.
7. Conduct a concluding ritual and blessing to remember our prophetic ancestors.

The psycho-social component

Thematic investigation... becomes a common striving towards awareness of reality and toward self-awareness.[49]

—Paulo Freire

Listening to the Earth

I suggested earlier that humans may function as the consciousness of the Earth, the psyche of the cosmos. The Psycho-Social component of Geo-Justice deals with the relationship of our minds and souls—our psyches—with global society. Each of us is a microcosm of the universe.

Where do we start? We might ask, "What is happening in my life that ignites my interest and passion?" Or, "In what ways is (or is not) my experience a liberating process that brings healing and balance to the Earth?"

As we approach the year 2000, we are increasingly aware of the vulnerability of the world that we know. Our planet is, as the media are beginning to acknowledge, an endangered planet. We are called to an awareness that puts both our own and our planet's vulnerability into perspective.

North America has, generally speaking, enshrined the rights of the individual at the expense of society. Robert Bellah wrote about this in *Habits of the Heart: Individualism and Commitment in American Life.*[50] Like Bellah, Geo-Justice rejects the "either/or" dichotomy between the individual and the group. Instead, it asserts "both/and"—the balance between psyche and society reflects the balance we can bring to the Earth. By cracking the "either/or" trap of having to choose between individual and social, personal and cultural, we can expand our personal awareness toward global healing. By listening to our psyches and to each other, we become better able to listen to society and to the Earth.

In earlier chapters, I referred to the need to connect the pain of the Earth to our own pain. This perception becomes a channel for healing. In the pain of the Earth and ourselves, we find inspiration and hope.

Hope comes from listening to the Earth. The Earth's story teaches a lesson of solidarity. The Earth's oppression is our own. Listening in silence, we become aware that we are not alone. Internal destructiveness is healed in hope, and systemic oppression is transformed to balance. The joy of this realization rescues us from loneliness and connects us to the Earth. In this connection, we contact the divine. We are both healers and healed.

A shift in consciousness

An important dimension of working for justice with the Earth is a shift in consciousness. As our awareness of the Earth deepens, we often undergo profound changes. An increasing number of people tell me they now see their connection to the Earth as the basis for their spiritual journey. They begin to view themselves, others, and the Earth in a new way.

This new consciousness is enhanced by making the connection between personal experience and the Earth's experience. The dialectic contributes to a new self-understanding. It supports a consciousness both transformative and transforming. The shift in awareness brings a new understanding of ourselves and the world.

The Psycho-Social dimension of Geo-Justice focuses on the connection between the person and society. When we perceive problems as either insoluble or nonexistent, we lapse into despair, apathy, and resignation. Rather than create solutions, we act out our unresolved problems. We create nuclear stockpiles; we compel the good Earth to do our will with massive doses of fertilizer and ever more powerful machinery.

The energy of our new awareness must be invested in transforming ourselves as well as structures and systems. We need both local and global perspectives, to unite our personal pain to the Earth's pain. Psychic healing becomes a microcosm of the healing of society. When we see the individual psyche linked with all of humanity and with the entire cosmos, every aspect of our lives becomes an instrument of planetary peace. Separateness and fragmentation are brought into balance.

From the perspective of Geo-Justice, the psyche's dynamic relationship to society integrates one's fragmented inner life to promote inner harmony and planetary peace.

Emotional integration

Historically, psychology and medicine have opted for the Cartesian and Newtonian paradigms—that is, a mechanical model of the universe. Once set in motion, the universe operated like a machine made up of many parts. The machine broke down only when a part failed. According to this view, healing happens when the part is repaired independently of the whole.

Psychology and medicine have traditionally assumed that the body and mind operate in a similar way. Mechanically understood, body and mind draw attention to themselves only when they are out of order. Mental health in this context idealizes tranquility and the *absence* of strong emotion. Even today, psychiatric hospitals depend on drug therapy to suppress (tranquilize) the patients' feelings.

By contrast, Geo-Justice values the healing potential of powerful feelings. A Geo-Justice psychology affirms Freud's approach of making the unconscious conscious, Jung's concept of befriending our shadow, and Robert Linder's assertion that personal psychological processes are instruments of cultural evolution.

Dr. Stan Grof, the prophetic psychiatrist, suggests that the release of the trapped energies of the psyche can be seen as a spiritual emergence—an opportunity for harmony and balance in the psyche. Grof suggests that the psyche itself is co-extensive with the universe. In *Beyond the Brain* he writes, "Modern consciousness research has added new levels, realms, and dimensions and shows the human psyche as being essentially commensurate with the whole universe and all of existence."[51]

Carl Jung, in an interview with Laurens van der Post on BBC

TV, commented: "When you look inside yourself, you see the universe and all its stars in all their infinity, objectively spaced out, and you fall away into an infinite symmetry, an infinite objective mystery within yourself, as great as the one without!"

When we can feel the pain of the Earth and identify it as our own pain, we can recognize that the psyche, in working towards its own healing and harmony, moves us all toward planetary justice, balance and peace.

New emphasis was put on recognition of spirituality and transcendental needs as intrinsic aspects of human nature and on the right of every individual to pursue his or her own spiritual path.[52]
—*Stan Grof*

Mapping the future

In therapy, past, present and future come together. How we respond to the present reveals a great deal about our past. Our response to any current crisis is conditioned by our responses to past crises. Our expectations of the future are either "more of the same" or "different from the past"; either way, those expectations are shaped by our history.

In attempting to provide therapy to the Earth, therefore, we do not start with a clean slate at square one. We can only proceed by realizing how we got here.

Healing and self-discovery are therefore not simply a constant mining of the past, a relentless plumbing of the depths of the seemingly infinite unconscious, a perpetual pursuit of unresolved material. They focus on meaning and purpose. They enable us to discover a perspective, a point of view, from which to determine our destiny. The patterns of the past provide a map for our journey. They enable us to reflect critically on our lives and to evaluate the best possible investment of energy for the future.

Toward unity and wholeness

Even as we experience the transformation of our world view, we are developing a new framework for understanding the psyche. Spectrum psychology envisages the psyche functioning in four different ways or channels. Each of these channels provides an avenue through which the organism can heal itself.

- Sensory Awakening—the activation and experiencing of all the senses.
- Biographical—recording of memories in the psyche; healing through remembering and reliving our experiences
- Perinatal Process—the experience before, during and after birth and the passage to new levels of experience.
- Transpersonal—the experience of moving beyond the confines of space and time, transcending the limited range of the senses as the source of new knowledge.

Stan Grof has developed an approach to activating the healing properties of the psyche which he calls **holonomic integration**. The name means moving toward unity and wholeness. It combines enhanced breathing with evocative music, focused body work, mandala drawing, and group sharing. This healing approach invites us simply to be, to support and to allow.

My own study of and participation in this process has been one of the most healing experiences of my life. I have also found holonomic integration to be very helpful in assisting the students with whom I work to experience deep levels of transformation. Their comments demonstrate how, given the right conditions, the psyche can experience healing.

- The time passed very quickly. I wasn't aware of it passing. At the end, I was very silent, very centered and did not want to do anything but just be quiet and centered. I was quite full when I left the experience.
- I felt deeply the various moods of music—sometimes stimulated to a very intense energy which I allowed my body to express as impelled; otherwise to a profound peace and restfulness. The overall effect seemed to be one of a sense of wholeness and contentment with who I am in the cosmos.
- I was going through some conflicts before the process, and

at the end of it the conflicts seemed negligible. Also got in touch with a certain anger toward my dad—that got dissolved, and now I feel a real closeness with him. It seems as if we're on a new plane of relationship.

The statements indicate that in such a process, spirituality and healing coincide. Together, they confirm that our inner psychological experience is dialectically connected to our social experience. Thus the psyche can be a source of Geo-Justice.

It is also true that our psychology is earth derived; diminution of the natural world is a diminution of the inner psychic world... The natural world is also a resource for our minds... When we extinguish these other life forms we being to lose our imagination and our refinement of emotion.[53]

—*Thomas Berry*

What we do to ourselves, we do to the Earth

These new approaches to psychology have enormous potential for balance and harmony on the Earth. To take just one example, research of the perinatal process has revealed that the experience of being trapped in the birth process evokes emotions that may later find expression in war. The task of psychology, as an instrument of Geo-Justice, is the creation of a safe place to detoxify our emotional poisons without harm to others or the Earth. Holonomic integration is one such approach.

In this view of the psyche, it is possible both to experience emotions fully and to contribute to transforming the planet. Self-exploration and expression will cleanse, purify and protect both ourselves and the planet. We will be less likely to act out hidden emotions. We will be able to mend the inner fragmentation of our lives and our alienation from the Earth. We will be able to experience each moment fully, without always having to move on to more ambitious plans and unlimited growth. We move from compulsion to peace.

In the 1960s, responding to the cultural moment and the promptings of my own questions, I began an adventure of self-discovery. In those days the question I asked was, "What are you angry about?" Today's question is, "What do you want to create together?"

I believed then and still believe today that the examination of one's emotional life is extremely important. What troubled me was that therapy and organizational work could be in dualistic isolation. Each failed to encompass the wisdom available from the other. One pursued emotional healing while overlooking oppressive structures, the other sought systemic change without dealing with personal need. My doctoral work focused on the need for a synthesis; from this experience I integrated the psycho-social component into the Geo-Justice paradigm. The opportunity to study with Stan Grof in the "Spiritual Emergence Network" provided deeper insights into the healing properties of the psyche.

Stan Grof writes that "a life and death struggle for survival gives way to a new image of a cosmic dance or divine play. The critical importance of synergy, cooperation, harmony, and ecological concerns is deeply felt and becomes self-evident."[54]

The Psycho-Social dimension of Geo-Justice invites us to recognize ourselves in relation to society. What we do to ourselves, we do to others and to the Earth. The alternative is equally true— as psychology can transform how we think, live and act, it becomes an instrument for Geo-Justice.

This kind of process, writes Stan Grof, "develops a new appreciation and reverence for all forms of life, and a new understanding of the unity of all things, which ... results in strong ecological concerns and greater tolerance toward other human beings. Consideration of all humanity, compassion for all life, and thinking in terms of the entire planet take priority over the narrow interests of individuals, families, political parties, classes, nations, and creeds. That which connects us all and that which we have in common become more important than our differences..."[55]

Process Reflection

In small groups ponder the following questions:

1. What in your life ignites your imagination and interest?
2. How do you see transformation in yourself contributing to transformation of the Earth?
3. What systems and structures in society (industry, politics, etc.) restrict your freedom of personal transformation?

In plenary group, consider the following questions:

4. What feelings did you experience as you shared and listened in the small groups?
5. How do you react to the notions of self-exploration? To social analysis? To the linking of the two?
6. How does this reflection enhance your understanding of the Psycho-Social component of Geo-Justice?

Closing ritual

Part IV

**A preferential option
for the Earth**

Toward a theology of Geo-Justice

The whole planet Earth, as an entirety, must also be seen as a context for theology... Today the destinies of all peoples are closely interrelated and linked to the future of the Earth: the land, the sea, the atmosphere and outer space.[56]

—*Tissa Balasuriya*

Building on liberation theology's "preferential option for the poor," Geo-Justice challenges us to a preferential option for the Earth.

This option invites us into a practical solidarity with the wounds of the Earth. In the struggle for global justice, we view the planet itself as victim. The planet is hungry, sick, devastated and dying. A preferential option for the Earth calls us to a theology rooted in the experience of global oppression, ecological devastation, and institutionalized resistance to social, gender, political, and economic equality. In solidarity, we see ourselves as part of the raped rainforests, abused children, marginalized women, and economically disadvantaged; we embrace our experience of interconnectedness with the poor and with the poor Earth. We awaken to the needs of the biosphere.

That solidarity, in turn, helps us discover that the needs of the Earth are one with our own deepest desires. That is the source of what I called "magnetic intuition." Thus a preferential option for the Earth honors the impulse to integrate the rhythm of our lives with the processes of the planet itself.

Through the process of theological reflection, Geo-Justice

makes us increasingly aware of the connection between our actions and what we most deeply believe in. Theological reflection releases enormous energy. By learning to listen to our inner promptings, we recognize God's creative energy as the source of personal and social transformation.

Theological reflection, in the context of Geo-Justice, explores the congruence between our mystical, prophetic and personal experiences and our global awareness, local action and societal vision. Theological reflection in Geo-Justice opens us to an operative theology of the Earth, a gospel view that sees the Earth as the poor, the voiceless, and the locus of divine action. Gustavo Gutiérrez, the liberation theologian from Peru, in his book *We Drink From Our Own Wells,* asserts that theological reflection builds on commitment and faith. Theological reflection challenges us to trust our imagination, as we apply our deepest experiences of awe, protest, and self-discovery to the concrete circumstances of our lives. It integrates what we most deeply trust with how we act. Theological reflection aligns faith and life; it brings to the surface an intuitive value system which gives meaning and purpose to our lives.

The practice of theological reflection, in the light of a preferential option for the Earth, ensures that the action that flows from our reflection will be responsive to the needs of the Earth. This reflection has three steps.

- We examine our deepest convictions, revealed in mysticism, prophecy, and personal experience.
- We seek a congruence between these convictions and our view of the Earth as the locus of the divine.
- We develop transformative actions to heal the Earth.

Such an approach to theological reflection is responsive both to our own experience and to the needs of the Earth. It will shed new light on our traditions, and encourage us to discover possibilities for action in every area of our lives. It prevents us from uncritically accepting imposed patterns of living and acting. Our reflections reveal the imbalances on the planet; prophetic impulses demand concrete action. As we connect these reflections with the Gospel, we develop an operative theology of the Earth.

From this experience of trusting the Earth and ourselves, a new language is born, new realizations awakened. We are empowered by the intentions of the Earth itself. We become instruments of healing the Earth and ourselves.

We live in a time when world trade, global communication, economic practices, science, technology, commerce and domestic life are all undergoing profound changes. This period has two characteristics: old ways of organizing experience no longer serve as accurate descriptions of the way things are; new ways of organizing experience can be confusing until a new world view emerges. Thus I say that an old order is dying and a new one is being born. We know that old structures are breaking down; we do not yet see clearly the shape of the new structures and possibilities.

Theologically, what is happening is nothing less than the intense and critical re-enactment of the Paschal mystery, the on-goingness of death and resurrection in our present moment. At this time, we are called to **think, pray** and **reflect theologically** about our place and response. We must not only cope, we must exercise capable, creative and competent leadership.

We **think**. Through reflection we deepen our spiritual journey. We see that what we most deeply believe is rooted in our tradition. We have an increased conviction that the divine permeates all of life, and that reverencing creation for its own sake is in fact an act of faith.

Strengthened by this awareness, we can explore the implications for our lives and for the Earth. As we reflect on our experiences in the light of faith, we search for resources that will increase our capacity to respond. We are invited to think about science, from which all peoples receive a common story of the Earth; about our faith, which perceives the Earth as God's unique creation; about our work, which is born in our hearts and minds from the needs of the Earth.

We **pray**. Prayer, in the context of Geo-Justice, consists of keeping our hearts and minds open to the beauty and crises of our time. We listen, so that we can respond creatively and courageously.

We **reflect theologically**. To theologize is to understand and articulate the connections between our deepest convictions and the work we are called to do. Making these connections releases enormous energy. It enables us to contribute more fully to healing the Earth.

From reflection, action

To exercise leadership in healing the wounds of the Earth is very much an act of faith. The call to this work is nourished by the roots of our tradition. It is a style of service that can expand our understanding of the Gospel, and can lead to new understandings that will invite us to even more creative responses.

The wisdom of the Christian tradition will help us to see these new understandings, these principles of healing the Earth, as harmonious with the Gospel.

Pentecost
May we all feel
A new sense of hope
A sense of peace, purpose and place
That what remains our fondest wish
Will be accomplished
By a wonderful connectedness
Of all that draws
Our energy, interest and talent
Bringing to life
What we most deeply know.

—*Conlon*

Healing
the Earth

...There is the feminine dimension of God which we identify with the Holy Spirit. She is the principle of communion, binding all reality together... All attraction, all bonding, all intimacy and communion flows from the Spirit.[57]

—*Sean McDonagh*

Pentecost reminds me of walking home at dusk in my small Ontario hometown. When the street lights went on, I suddenly could see those whom I would meet.

Pentecost happens whenever "the lights go on," whenever people realize they are not walking alone. When I invite people at a Geo-Justice workshop to find someone they don't know and to share what is important to them, they almost always report a wonderful experience of interconnectedness with the other person. This healing of separation is the experience of Pentecost.

Musically, harmony involves blending individual notes into a common chord. Science teaches us that the universe is a symphony of harmony and balance, each part of the universe interdependent with every other part. This offers an auditory image of Pentecost. Often, in Geo-Justice groups, I ask each person to hum a particular note. Research indicates that the Earth vibrates at C-sharp. When we all hum C-sharp, we are not only in resonance with each other but with the Earth as well. The resulting sound always reminds us powerfully of unity and peace.

I also often ask people to draw their own mandala for a planetary

Pentecost. Always, the figures they create represent harmony, unity, interdependence.

These images of Pentecost in word, sight, and sound become indicators of things coming together on Earth.

Pain and paradox

We live today in a time of great pain. Our cities are wracked with senseless violence. Our rivers are poisoned, our lakes suffer from acid rain. Our atmosphere chokes on greenhouse gases. More than at any other time in the past 20 centuries, the Earth reflects Paul's words to the Romans: "...the whole creation has been groaning as in the pains of childbirth..."[58]

This pain carries great hope for a planetary Pentecost, a new way of living together on the planet. The problems are all related; so are the solutions. Just as in that moment at dusk when the street lights are turned on and the darkness of isolation ends, we can now see everything as interconnected, woven together.

In Geo-Justice, we recognize anew our capacity to be instruments of healing and justice. An awareness of our personal pain, united to the pain of the cosmos, becomes a basis for our work. Connecting to cosmic pain energizes psychic balance, cosmic harmony, and compassion. By getting in touch with our pain for the outrage perpetrated on the Earth, we generate energy to throw off the blanket of inertia that stifles creative action and that promotes resignation and despair.

We feel freed to act, at our own level, in our own situation. As we act, we participate in healing the Earth. If we allow the pain we feel to be simply personal, it can be limiting, separating, and isolating. Geo-Justice challenges us to move to a cosmic level. It is an important moment for the Earth and for ourselves.

Geo-Justice emerges from the dynamic of the Earth itself. The process is geological, biological, and human. It invites a reflection on the role of people within the universe. It reminds us to let go of domination and move toward participation in the harmony already present in the universe. Geo-Justice depends less on our being initiators than participants, members of the gigantic chorus that permeates and flows into all aspects of existence. Geo-Justice finds expression in the equity and relationship of all creation.

As we move into the 21st century, we imagine new ways of taking responsibility for our life and for the world, for living out our preferential option for the Earth. We re-vision ways to restructure society and to transform the various forms of oppression that we experience. Geo-Justice invites us to be people of justice, instruments of harmony, participants in balance, promoters of interconnectivity, and healers of the ruptures in the fabric of creation that cause injustice for psyche, society and the planet.

The development of such a theology is an undertaking of praxis—a synthesis of action and reflection. It focuses first on the ongoing Pentecost event, and sees how the creative energy of God is expressed in and through the energy of the Earth. The Pentecost event identifies our work of healing the Earth as an expression of divine creative energy. Richard McBrien, in *Catholicism*, writes of this energy which "heals, reconciles, renews, gives life, bestows peace, sustains hope, brings joy, and creates unity; the principle of communion binding all things together in one nurturing enveloping embrace, healing what is broken, reuniting what is separate and recreating the face of the Earth."[59]

When we get in touch with our deepest convictions and find them congruent with the roots of our faith, we will generate a genuine enthusiasm for life and a preferential option for the Earth.

The key to Pentecost is an awakening from our depths. A planetary Pentecost is the deepening and expansion of this healing moment for the Earth in our time. It affirms life and confirms the goodness of the Earth.

The planetary perspective makes possible a vision that takes us beyond ourselves to see the world in a new way. Healing the Earth will also heal us. As Thomas Berry said: "We *are* the Earth."

The cultural context

The movement toward a theology of Geo-Justice will be shaped by the context where it occurs. Geo-Justice in Latin America will not be the same as in North America, in Europe as in South Africa. Because different regions liberate and oppress the Earth in different ways, each must respond differently. The industrialized nations may need to work at an ecological or economic response; others, a political response or social revolution.

We should not expect from this movement toward a planetary Pentecost a theology worked out in advance. This theology will evolve in practice. We admire the beauty of the Earth; we listen to its pain; we act out our preferential option for the Earth; we reflect on the state of our planet, in light of what we most deeply trust is true. Thus we develop a theology of Geo-Justice.

This theology will emerge into our consciousness. Its discovery will flood us with gratitude for all that we have received from the Earth. Thus we will understand more deeply the meaning of planetary Pentecost for our day.

We live in an important time, a time of hope, of struggle and of Geo-Justice. We live in a time when the dominant culture and some dimensions of organized religion militate against justice and change. We live in a time when religious language can be put to the service of the status quo, when a disembodied spirituality can subtly oppress people and justify the unjust. Never has the call to work and destiny been so much a call to *Geo*-Justice.

An adaptation of a statement from the 1971 Bishops' Synod describes a preferential option for the Earth, and its operative theology: "Action on behalf of the Earth, and participation in the restoration, development and transformation of the global environment fully appears as a constitutive dimension of the Gospel—the healing of the cosmos and its deliverance from every oppressive situation."

An outline for theological reflection

I have found the following process to work well in groups.

1. **Biographical and Descriptive Phase**. In a group, participants discuss:
   - Who they are and their pressing global, local and personal concerns;
   - What they perceive the problems to be;
   - What they have done about these problems up to now;
   - What is needed to resolve the problems/concerns as perceived.

2. **Thematic Phase.**
   - What themes emerge from the biographical and descriptive process?

3. Synthesis Phase.
- How do we "get a handle" on the areas of primary concern? Build a list of specific issues. These should be recognizable, concrete expressions of the theme and should present the question from many perspectives. Possible vehicles could be stories, photos, mime, statements, etc.

4. Analytical Phase.
Participants view the themes, using them as a lens to develop a deeper and more comprehensive understanding of the issues. The analytical phase involves responding to questions such as these:
- Perception: What do you see that relates to your lives? How does it make you feel?
- Personal experience: What do you know about this from your life?
- Group experience: What similarities from personal experiences begin to be recognized by the whole group?
- Larger context: What is the larger picture that your experience is part of? What are the global, local and personal implications?
- Action: What are appropriate actions to take from the perspective of Geo-Justice?
- Critique: How are our proposed actions congruent with or contradictory to the needs of the Earth from a Gospel perspective?

Practices in Geo-Justice

We cannot create knowledge without acting. The focus of this action is (a) to transform the world, (b) to establish inter-dependent relationships with human beings, with the cosmos and with God.[60]

—*Paulo Freire*

Education

Education has become a vehicle for social conformity. But true education does not impose predetermined responses; it does not oppress; it is a place to reflect critically on what emerges from within. True education involves making sense and gaining perspective, not merely assimilating others' information. We create knowledge, we do not simply absorb it.

Hildegard of Bingen defined education, long ago, as a celebration of our capacity to reflect, to look at ourselves, and to be critical of ourselves and our work.[61] Today we could say that education is about being open to the wisdom and treasures of the earth.

The creation of knowledge is organic and liberating. It frees us from imposed patterns and presuppositions. In fact, when I facilitate groups on Geo-Justice, I often find it helpful to present the components of Geo-Justice as *sources of knowledge*. As groups present and reflect on their response to these components, they ignite the act of learning. They create their own knowledge of Geo-Justice.

As educators know, learning takes place most effectively when the curriculum grows out of the students' interests. Such students are self-motivated; they want to see the connection of their own experience with the subject being studied.

Since Geo-Justice involves reflecting on the connections between individual experience and society, global and local action, and the Earth, it is an appropriate vehicle for education. This sequence is patterned after the work of Paulo Freire, the Brazilian pedagogue.[62]

1. Generate and record an overview of themes that matter to the participants: listen to their motivations, hopes, feelings, and needs.
2. Represent those themes in the form of "codes." In preparing a "code" we convert abstract ideas or themes into a drawing or picture, and accompany it with a statement.
3. Have participants reflect critically on their experience through personal and group responses to the codes. Follow that reflection with appropriate research and/or actions.

In one of my classes, the first step generated the following "themes."

- Increased hope through a re-emergence of a social conscience manifested by a concern for nuclear disarmament, beauty and environmental concerns.
- Spiritual awakening among people who revere creation for its own sake.
- Breakthrough into an understanding of creativity, and of practising it in our culture.
- Movement beyond what is comfortable and known.
- Actions for freedom which affirm ethnicity, multiculturalism, and actively confront the dualisms of our cultural life.[63]

In the second step, we expressed those themes visually, visibly—not simply as abstract words. We created pictures, images and dramatizations, of emergence, of awakening, of breakthrough, of freedom from fear, of confrontation. We accompanied these illustrations with a brief statement. As we looked at these coded messages, literal and visual representations of our experience, we began to understand ourselves and the world in a new way.

The "codes" generated questions for reflection in Step 3: Who do you see? How does it make you feel? What do you know about it from your life? What are the group responses? How is your story and the group experience related to the larger global context? What research is needed to further our understanding? What are the implications for action on behalf of Geo-Justice?

Educator and activist Parker Palmer has commented: "Good teaching is often about helping people learn things they already know but don't know that they know."[64] Similarly, Freire says that the goal of education is not simply to know, but to *know* that you know. Two years after participating in such a session, a woman sent me a reflection she had written that reflects this understanding of education. She wrote: "It has been quite a while since I was in your class but the experience is still so vivid to me that in some ways it was only yesterday. I want to thank you for affirming me in what I already knew. And the mantra that came to me that week is still with me:

> "I know that I know that I know
> I know that I know that I know
> I know that I know
> I know that I know
> I know that I know that I know that I know."

Social analysis means raising questions about society and seeking answers. Its purpose is not only to develop a critical awareness of the world but also to head towards social justice.[65]

—*Michael Czerny S.J. and Jamie Swift*

Social analysis: from resignation to hope

We live in a mystifying and highly complex society. Moment by moment we are confronted with a dual option: either there are no problems, or the problems seem so enormous that we can't do anything about them. Mass market media and merchandising don't help; they invite us to further distortion, desperation, and despair.

Yet, somewhere within us, and within the cosmos, are the seeds of diagnosis and resolution. We feel a growing hope, an increasing conviction that we *can* make sense out of the problems of the planet. We *can* and *must* move toward constructive and creative action for the new society about to be born.

Today we do not need more people telling us what is wrong, nor what to do to obtain "instant relief" from particular problems. We do not need more of the kind of education that turns students into banks in which to deposit knowledge. We need the opportunity to make sense of our world. We need a context where we can diagnose problems, reflect on them in light of our values, and initiate action congruent with our world view. We need an analysis that can give us direction for our journey, that can help us reflect on our interaction with the political, economic, and social structures of daily life.

The book *Getting Started in Social Analysis in Canada* [66] invites you to reflect on your last purchase or meal. Where was it purchased? Who made the cereal, juice or coffee that you ate for breakfast? How was it distributed? Who profited? How are decisions about the manufacture and marketing made? What does the product you ate have to say about your lifestyle?

By focusing such questions around a product and its relationship to systems and structures, we practise social analysis. Remember that analysis from the perspective of the Earth does not try to comprehend the whole by examining its parts. Something new operates here: an understanding of the whole as whole. Through such an analysis, we no longer see our actions as a private matter, but interconnected through a network of relationships with the whole world.

In common usage, the term "analysis" often reveals a bias for viewing life from a parts perspective. Psychoanalysis traditionally has dealt with the psyche as separate from the family and the social system. Social analysis has often looked at society without considering the global dimension of problems. Global efforts have often overlooked the local and psychological aspects of inquiry. Geo-Justice offers an analytical perspective that embraces all three components in the context of the whole.

This is an important contribution. It significantly shifts our understanding of analytical categories. Questions about power, decision-making, and compromise all make us aware of our political experience from a planetary perspective. Looking at our ethnic roots, our denominational ties, our relationship to beauty, art, and celebration, we begin to understand our cultural experience and move toward an ecological consciousness. Questions about money, work, goods, and their influence on privatization and compassion move us to explore the economy. Whatever the area, as we move from random questioning toward an examination of our relationship to the structures of society, we develop a social analysis.

Social analysis can be described as an approach to understanding our relationship to the systems of society in order to transform them. It particularly helps us to focus on aspects of relationships that may be oppressive. Oppression can be named as the systematic denial of choices and opportunities for persons and groups. Social analysis therefore becomes the key to unlocking liberation. Once we understand where and how freedom is denied to us, we begin to know where and how to bring about change. This approach to freedom awakens us from unconsciousness and paralysis. It encourages us to trust our intuitions and feelings and to participate in Geo-Justice by transforming oppressive structures.

One indicator of this approach to liberation is the formation of unlikely coalitions. Individuals and groups who may come from opposite poles of a political spectrum will willingly cooperate on one issue, while realizing that on other issues they may disagree. An example might be women's groups that support each other in opposing pornography while holding radically different views on the rights of the unborn.

Social analysis has its limitations, however. It is a diagnosis, not a treatment. It reveals what is wrong in society. It does not solve the problem.

The dynamics of society

So how do we promote action for justice and transformation? Even more important, how do we overcome the blindness and despair that keep us from seeing what is wrong, and that keep us from generating enough hope to do something about it? Paulo Freire called himself the "Vagabond of the Obvious"[67] because he realized that deep within people's psyches lies a mystification, a blindness, an incapacity to see what's wrong so that they can do something about it. Peggy Way, long ago in Chicago, called Saul Alinsky the "Therapist of the Apathetic" because she realized, as did he, that resignation and despair immobilize us and hold us back from transformative action.

The transformation generated by social analysis is psycho-social; "psycho-" because it deals with the *feelings* that immobilize us and cause us to be outraged; "social" because it helps us to see where to direct the energies generated by our analysis. It involves both personal and structural transformation. It holds emotional and societal experience in a dialectical relationship.

"Dialectical" simply means that two different dimensions of experience belong together in tension. It is "both/and" not "either/or." The danger comes when we concentrate on one and exclude the other. The opposite of "dialectical" is "dualism"; this implies an experience of separateness, of subject/object relationships.

If we focus only on the psyche/mind, we run the risk of leaving out the context of the whole. In this approach we may resolve our emotional problems but fail to acknowledge the systemic roots of these problems in our society. Conversely, if we spend our time exploring the outward, systemic reality without acknowledging its interconnections with the psyche, we may project our unresolved emotional problems into our social action. The Psycho-Social approach to change enables us to work towards healing the psyche and society in a unified way.

Self-interest is the key to the dynamics of society. Properly understood, self-interest is about trust—trust that what is deepest and most wonderful to a person is inherently compatible with dignity and respect for all creation.

Two of the greatest social animators of our time, Alinsky and Freire, both based their work on a profound conviction that people genuinely wanted to do what was best for them and for society. Freire invited us to abandon our position of privilege, and to become united with the oppressed in working for freedom. Alinsky invited us to go beyond the limits of our immediate vision and to unite our energies for transformation and change. Alinsky said of this approach "And yet with all of this there is that wonderful equality of man [sic] that from time to time floods over the natural dams of survival... these episodic transfigurations of the human spirit."[68]

If indeed we are coded for compassion, then by trusting our intuition we will come to know what needs to be done. First we have to trust ourselves enough to contact the problem; then we need to perceive the problem in such a way that we can act to resolve it.

In the language of Alinsky, this is turning a problem into an issue and getting a handle on it. By naming an issue, we move from bewilderment to critical awareness. Thus, as we move from the fuzzy general problem of community health, to the specific issue of toxic chemicals dumped in Love Canal, we channel our energies for transformation.

Developing the practice of social analysis

The development of the practice of social analysis is like learning a new language. It is the process of becoming literate in "reading" reality.

Think for a moment of your childhood, or of travelling as an adult to a foreign land. Remember the experience of not being able to understand the language. You can have an acute sense of alienation, of being cut off and unable to function. Social illiteracy, the inability to read our social reality, is equally a handicap. Without social analysis, you can find yourself constantly mystified by what's going on around you. Things just don't make sense. Complexities overwhelm you. This can often lead to despair.

Social analysis develops our social literacy to increase our awareness and our hope. It leads to strategizing for action. In Latin America this process of moving from analysis to action is called conjunctural analysis—an assessment of the interrelationship of forces, be they political, economic, social, or ideological. The movement from analysis to action involves four steps:
- identifying interests,
- naming the issues,
- assessing the forces,
- planning action.

A Canadian project, The Jesuit Centre for Social Faith and

Justice, calls this movement, "Naming the Moment."[69] "Naming the Moment" starts by gathering people who are working in different ways to solve social problems. These might include social workers, church people, community people, academics, and others. They come together to:

- reflect on the different forces affecting the community;
- identify issues to decide which way to proceed;
- open up questions which arise from various perspectives, and explore possible actions to initiate change;
- assess the dominant forces at play in the most important issues of a given moment;
- conduct a short- and medium-range assessment of possibilities;
- determine opportunities for action.

People involved in this process are already at work on social problems. Whatever action results from the process assists the various groups and movements to work in harmony. Part of that goal is achieved simply by drawing the people together, to develop a common vision and strategy.

The Geo-Justice tree

From the Jesuit "Naming the Moment" project, I have adapted the Geo-Justice Tree. It is a way of visualizing how the components of social structures interrelate in the work of Geo-Justice. The Geo-Justice Tree has four components: roots, trunks, branches, and leaves.

- *Roots*: The economic system at the base of the social structure; integration of human production, distribution and consumption, within the context of Earth as our home.
- *Trunk*: The organizational, political, and planetary systems that make the system run.
- *Branches*: The social organization sand institutions; that provide balance between humans and the environment.
- *Leaves*: The ideological aspects of society; its beliefs and values, and its structures for transmitting them such as schools, churches, and media. The spiritual aspects of global community—beliefs, values and structures for

100

transmitting a sense of the sacred in all creation.

The four components exist in relation to each other. No tree bears leaves without a trunk, or branches without roots. The economic system to a large extent determines the kind of political system. The ideological pattern of beliefs and values reinforces and critiques the economic and social system. Our social and political organizations support the status quo in both economics and ideology. As a metaphor, the tree shows us how each of these parts relates to each other part.

The metaphor of the tree encourages us to see that action for justice cannot be separated from spirituality. Native peoples viewed the universe from the perspective of the four elements: earth, air, water, and fire. The tree interacts with all these elements. It cannot live if uprooted from the earth, or if deprived of air or water or fire (sun). The elements of the universe are thus the context of the tree.

In a group, one might follow this process:

- Introduce the Geo-Justice tree with a drawing, linking the four aspects of society with the four parts of the tree;
- Divide the participants into four working groups, one each for the roots, trunk, branches, and leaves;
- Each group takes on its own tasks, brainstorming around major issues of the moment from its own economic, social, political or ideological perspective;
- Each group chooses and discusses one issue from its list and writes down its key findings;
- The whole group reconvenes to report the results of its discussions, with each group taping its issue onto the drawing of the tree and explaining its choice.
- In plenary, the whole group discusses the four issues selected and compares them: How are they related? Where do they converge? Do they represent aspects of the same issue?
- The whole group moves toward a consensus on which issue to organize around.
- Finally, the group "names" the issue. This name should not be simply some abstract generalization, like "nuclear disarmament" or "protection of the environment." The issue

selected should be as specific as possible. It should lend itself to concrete action and resolution. The process concludes by assessing the best opportunities for organizing, and the action each group is willing to take.

This process enables participants to move from complacency to interest, from mystification to cultural awareness, from resignation to hope. It enables participants to see their analysis from the perspective of Geo-Justice.

> We are challenged to fashion life-giving lives and be co-creators with the Divine ... through our service to the world, our lives are transformed.[70]
>
> —*Jane Blewett*

Working groups

The relationship of the person to the group is critical to the dynamic of the transformative process. The participant is a microcosm of the collective. What each person thinks or feels affects the group and reflects its perceptions. Even when a person expresses an opinion that is not shared by others, that view influences the views of the others (positively or negatively) and at the same time indicates the range of views held within the group as a whole.

For this reason, the coordinator of any group encourages participants to get in touch with themselves, to become aware of the emotional material that resides within. This is often facilitated by being aware of breathing, becoming conscious of one's body, and avoiding the distractions of trivial conversation. From this examined silence, group members are invited to speak.

This approach develops a collective consciousness that strengthens the group's capacity to function together. They don't have to agree; they do have to communicate openly and honestly with each other. The participation of any group member will, on some level, both express the group's experience and articulate others' experience.

The facilitator's primary function is to prevent behavior that could be destructive. This possibility needs to be taken seriously. In contacting their inmost selves, group members are also potentially in touch with personality factors that could oppress others.

At the same time, the facilitator encourages the group to develop a collective consciousness, a group mind. This group mind energizes the group interaction. The facilitator assists the group to identify where the pressure is, who is most in need of speaking; the facilitator guides the discussion from one member's shared experience to another's.

These dynamics apply to any group. But not all groups function the same way. For some, the dynamic for action comes from within the group itself; others get their dynamic from external sources.

Traditionally, from the Newtonian-Cartesian perspective, group process involved setting an agenda and moving towards a goal in an orderly way. This is a linear approach to group work. It's predictable and effective for accomplishing tasks. But the process discourages creative expression within the group.

It is not often understood that within any group is an energy mass. The group process should encourage this energy to unfold. When this happens, the group becomes self-energizing and self-organizing.

People do not always welcome self-organizing groups. Such groups have a tendency to get away from pre-planned agendas, to take matters into their own hands. They can no longer be controlled. For Geo-Justice, of course, that is precisely what is desired. External control is the antithesis of the Geo-Justice process.

Any self-energizing and self-organizing group will experience a critical moment. This moment can transform the group. Or it can erode the collective energy. The group facilitator tries to ensure that the energy released by the group process can be channeled toward transformation, neither imploding back upon the group destructively nor exploding outside the group in a chaotic and ineffectual outpouring.

In my experience, the energy that emerges from this critical moment will express itself in one or more of the three components of Geo-Justice: global, local, or psycho-social. That is, it will focus on awareness of unity, action at a local level, or personal change.

Much will depend on the kind of stories that the participants have been telling each other. From the outset, participants should have the opportunity to tell stories about what is most important to them, and what they celebrate as a sign of effectiveness in their work. In doing so, they make connections between their relationship to the Earth and their own work.

If their stories have focused on self-discovery or societal change, the group will probably concentrate on the Psycho-Social component of Geo-Justice. If their stories have told about taking action on a specific issue, they will gravitate towards prophetic global and local action. And if their experiences have been of oneness with the beauty of ultimate reality, of spirituality, they will choose primarily the component of global mysticism for moving forward into the future.

At this point in the process, the group's energy is focused; they want, they expect, something new to happen. The result can be new structures and forms for organizing themselves, coupled with a new collective awareness.

Process reflection

1. How has your experience of education, social analysis and group work been an expression of justice-making?
2. What other vehicles are available to you in your life for the practice of Geo-Justice?
3. How does your experience of mysticism, prophecy, and self-discovery enable you to participate in the practice of Geo-Justice?

Part V

The emergence of a planetary Pentecost

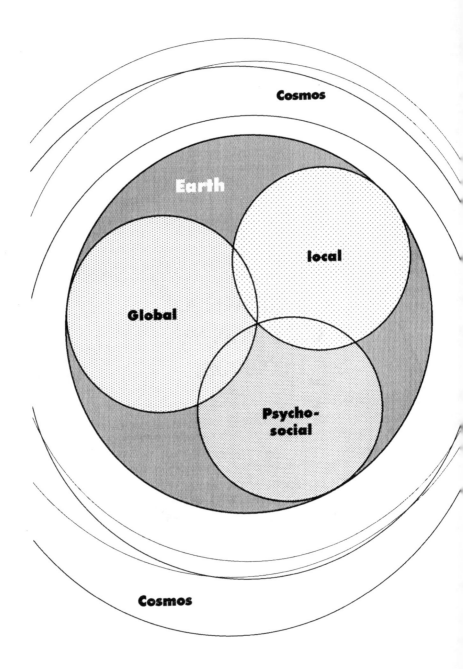

Exploring the mandala

A synoptic diagram that contains the important events of the Earth in a condensed and stylized way ...[71]

—*Adapted from Stan Grof*

A mandala is a graphic symbol for the universe, usually in some circular form. It is helpful to explore such a symbol as a means of establishing through visual imagery some of the elements of Geo-Justice that I have discussed in this book.

The circle is a good starting point. It is, first of all, an image from the cosmos, the shape of the Earth, which is the context for Geo-Justice. The circle reminds us of what may be the most powerful image any of us have ever seen—that glimpse of an ethereal blue-green ball of life floating in the impenetrable black void of space, our Earth as seen from outer space.

Within this circle, the components in the mandala for Geo-Justice complement each other. In the dynamics of Geo-Justice, there are no isolated or separated parts. Each component is a dimension of the whole. The components I have described all relate to each other within the mandala (circle)—the Global, the Local, and the Psycho-Social. In the next chapter, I describe how these three components work together to become "A Window For the World."

In that context, the circle also resembles a lens that we look

107

through to see more clearly. As we grasp the significance of each component in relation to the whole, the mandala for Geo-Justice becomes a lens to critique our approach to justice-making.

We need to keep in mind that we use the mandala as a working hypothesis. The experience of applying the mandala can alter and reinvent it. The students in my classes and workshops continually come up with new variations of the mandala that reflect their insights into the way Geo-Justice works.

The appendix of this book includes a list of organizations whose work is particularly attuned to the focus of Geo-Justice. By engaging in such Geo-Justice projects, we deepen our understanding of the components and of the sources from which Geo-Justice draws its wisdom. We will also be able to envision what remains to be revealed about those same components and sources. Action and reflection help to further refine and implement a framework for harmony and balance; a continuing critique opens us to the unfolding process of justice for the Earth.

Working with a mandala is not like working with a recipe or a handbook. What I offer, from research and reflection, is a visual framework, a symbolic checklist, a paradigm for the work of healing the Earth. Properly understood and experienced, these components (seen through the symbolic lens of the mandala) ensure that Geo-Justice is taking place. The mandala may also reveal that one component is currently lacking from a project. For example, local action may be enhanced by including self-knowledge or the global perspective.

The components of Geo-Justice can be understood as a symbolic map for bringing about global peace. The work of Geo-Justice can take place within the framework of any of these components or can move from one to the other. The process of Geo-Justice can be understood sometimes through the Global component, and at other times through the Local or the Psycho-Social components, or any combination of these, or all three.

A window for the world

> The strange, beautiful thing is that probably this time the vision will not be the product of any one person but will be a collective product. It will be the creation of a new human species as a macro-organism, as a perfected neural system made up of thousands and thousands of networks.[72]
>
> *Robert Muller*

A vision for the new millennium

Like Martin Luther King, Jr., I have a dream. I dream that the final decade of this millennium will lead us into a new kind of world in the coming millennium. This new era will put us in touch with our origins; it will dissolve alienation and promote creativity and peace. Instead of competing for power-over, we will work to build a better world by following a vision of beauty, love, laughter and peace. Our vision will permeate the coming culture and will invite each of us "to do whatever needs to be done."

A friend described this dream as the possibility of a corporate meeting without hierarchy, of winners without losers, of art without elitism, and of living ritual without boredom.

The concept of Geo-Justice offers the kind of vision that enables that kind of world to happen. It provides a "Window for the World." A Geo-Justice class, reflecting on the theme "Window for the World," generated these statements.

- We see a vast evolution of healing in which we participate by giving birth to our deepest passions;
- We see all people and creatures telling their stories and

109

listening to each other;
- We see that the responsibility lies with us;
- We see all people as the human heart of a healthy cosmos, in a new era of love, justice and service;
- We see people waking up to a new vision of creation, where humans will find their place among the species of the Earth and live in peace and harmony with all of creation;
- We see a world without private property laws, fences, window-guards, and instead with welcome signs to all to come and enjoy the Earth;
- We see that "ordinary people" see that the old paradigm is really failing and they are ready for the work of building a new world;
- We see people living and working in harmony with one another;
- We see products produced because they are needed, and as near to the place of consumption as possible;
- We see a precious present;
- We see men and women waking each day to sing their hearts' desire;
- We see God in each other;
- We see work to do;
- We see systems based on true partnership forged by mutual compassion;
- We see all people sharing together in creating a more just world, nurturing the ecology and building a healthy, peaceful future for generations to come;
- We see a world in which all people will have ample opportunity to grow to their fullest potential—a world free of war, full of respect and reverence for all creation.

The birth of a movement

The Geo-Justice vision is giving birth to a new consensus among people with diverse histories, denominations, languages and cultures. The process moves people toward a holistic world view. From the hot coals of a dying culture, we draw the fire of knowledge that comes from the heart, that fuels us with mysticism and prophecy for our journey.

Geo-Justice gives birth to our fondest hopes for the planet. This hope provides a window of opportunity for a truly global network and for a process that will utilize and integrate existing networks as partners in a Pentecost for the planet. It will enable existing groups to transcend their present organizational sovereignty.

The first task for leaders of this global event will be to develop imaginative ways to translate the vision of Geo-Justice into the lives of all people on this planet. We are called to quilt together a tapestry of relationships many would call a "Cosmic Fire-Web"; it gives cultural expression to the dynamics of the universe by being autonomous, interconnected, and self-organizing. We need what Thomas Berry has called "a human way of entering into the rhythms of the universe."[73]

Most people have traditionally viewed what happens to them as having significance only in their own lives. They need a perspective that sees cultural and personal events as expressions of the dynamics of the universe itself. They need to develop a cosmological imagination.This is a transformation of enormous magnitude. I believe the beginning of this transformation is already happening, all around the world. Leaders are called to promote and nurture what is already taking place.

Through this process, participants are reminded that they are not alone, and that there is no agenda but the "people's agenda."

This process gives birth to an entirely different kind of organization, which can best be described as the non-organization. Non-organizations are informal networks of information, support, and possible common action. They share a vision, and they often work together towards common goals. The development of these informal non-organizations is transforming how we see life and the Earth.

Their common vision is aligned to the work of Geo-Justice. Through these networks, these non-organizations, we are developing a window for the world, a new way of seeing and acting in the world. This movement ushers in a new era, a conscious shift toward peace for the planet. Action programs aligned with Geo-Justice principles are being developed. In-depth reflection is occurring. People feel connected to a focus of action. An intuitive awareness of Geo-Justice gives their diverse work a sense of interconnection.

A global coalition

The network of these non-organizations is becoming more explicit. The links grow out of the depths of people's lives and the pain of the Earth.

The Toronto *Globe and Mail* said that the birth of a movement "resembles nothing so much as the coming of spring; suddenly, spontaneously, everywhere the sap is rising, the trees and buds are swelling." A movement for peace with the Earth emerges from a common vision and the diversity of concrete action.

Bioregional base groups provide a vehicle for bringing about an ever-increasing critical mass of people moving from separation to oneness and empowerment. As they link together, a growing number of peacemakers will discover increased harmony within and balance without. Through analysis, strategy, and action, the focus of these groups is on peace with the earth. The recognition that we live with an uncertain future evokes the response of a cultural movement offering gifts to heal the Earth.

This movement encompasses the Earth. Through it, the Earth is becoming an "organism of oneness." The animators of this awakening are people who grow organically from their own history and traditions. They are willing to be seen, in the words of Gregory Baum and Duncan Cameron, as "far out, marginalized from seats of power, idealistic, irresponsible, naive or, at least ahead of their time."[74]

As we reflect on the signs of the times, we will see how each of us can contribute to a framework of hope. Because Geo-Justice does not depend on power-over but on co-operation and power-within, Geo-Justice is increasingly a pursuit of peace and an experience of oneness. In the words of James Bevel, "a movement is when people live what they sing about."[75] The work of Geo-Justice is more and more an affirmation of these words.

Seeing the new soul of our world

The eyes of children are windows both to our souls and to a new world. In children's eyes, we see our present world reflected; through their eyes, we see our future.

Similarly, Geo-Justice stands as a window to a world that is growing in cohesion and consciousness. The vision of Geo-Justice lets us see the soul of our own world more clearly, and helps us see what our world must become if it is to survive.

When we look at the world through the eyes of Geo-Justice, we are challenged. We see the goal, if not all the steps along the way. To reach that goal, we must walk through the labyrinth of our narrowness, sometimes unable to perceive more than one step at a time, trusting that we shall eventually emerge with a renewed consciousness and vision. The challenge comes in letting go of those areas that imprison our imaginations, that lock away our creativity, that prevent us from rising out of our ruts.

As we explore and express our participation in Geo-Justice as members of a movement and creators of a window for the world, we recognize our need for resources for our journey. I suggest that the following could be three important resources:

1. Personal links through written or oral communication. In the "non-organization" model, these links start with the individual who talks with others and writes letters. Through reflection and action together, groups can further the growth of Geo-Justice. These spontaneous activities can be focused through a "views letter" that provides personal **information** about gifts and needs and is a vehicle for growing articulation of the theory and practice of Geo-Justice.

2. Resource centers provide **support**, where written and recorded resources can be generated and exchanged. Geo-Justice workers can gather at such centers, re-vision their work, and develop programs for others. Some of these centers already exist: the Appendix lists a number of projects, people and places. The Bibliography lists some of the resources currently available in print.

3. Responsible **action**: participants in the movement are encouraged to respond individually, as a group, and in cooperation with other like-minded people. They benefit from each other's experience; they lend and receive support.

A vision statement created by a Regional Connectors for Base Groups in Creation Spirituality group identifies well the way that Geo-Justice can become a Window for the World.

Each of us and all that is
Is a unique word
Uttered with meaning and love
From the living heart of the universe.
We flow with one life
But speak with many voices.
We vow to cherish our common life
And hear its many voices,
So that together
We may sing
The song of the earth,
That echoes and calls forth
The gift of each
For the good of all.

Here is part of another vision statement proposed by a working group in a Geo-Justice class.

In relationship to myself: I seek to live with compassion, discipline and love. I will strive to embrace my shadow selves. I will continue my daily spiritual practice, striving to unite with my divine Goddess/God within.

In relationship to our group: We will continue to feel the support of companions travelling similar paths. We will write each of our companions at the winter and spring solstices, sharing reflections of our journey.

In relationship to our human brothers and sisters, we seek to:

See each one as he/she is by withdrawing our projections from them

Celebrate the dreams of the child in each one by listening open-heartedly

Honor and respect the evolving ability in each one to define and find their own way

In relationship to other species: We seek to remember our interconnectedness and interdependencies in our daily actions, living on our common home.

In relationship to institutions: We seek to remember institutions are assemblages of persons employed to serve a public of which we are a part. We will strive to take responsibility to claim our personal power when interacting with various institutions.

In relationship to the Earth: We will strive to remember that we are Earth; we are one living organism. We will continue living in the wonder of life with conscious awareness. We commit ourselves to change our habits in living on our home. We will live as ecologically and as lightly as possible.

An act of commitment

Geo-Justice is remembering that we are an integral part of the Earth community.

Geo-Justice commits us to a deepening awareness of Earth and all her life forms.

This means taking time
to play in and with the universe
to see,
hear,
feel,
touch,
taste,
celebrate.

Geo-Justice further commits us
to nurture,
to protect,
to defend
Earth and all her life forms.

Geo-Justice commits us
to live gratefully,
to live passionately,
and to hold sacred all being.

We will strive to live out this commitment.

Process Reflection
1. Present music and slides—pictures of the eyes of children.
2. Present the challenge—to be people who see differently.

115

3. Dramatize the transformation:
   - Cover your eyes with a mask, or your head with a paper bag. Imagine a journey to a vantage place; climb to a point where you can "see forever..."
   - Let go of a limited view: from this imaginary vantage place, pull off your masks, and toss them into the center, announcing what you are letting go of.
4. Develop a statement on Your Window for the World—in groups, create a song, poem, dance, or prose expression of your understanding of "Window for the World."
5. Ritual—in a circle, dance around your masks of limited view. Then re-vision into a Window to the World—form into the shape of a window and announce a collective statement for a Window to the World while looking into and through the window.
6. Form a circle of participants. Distribute balls of different colored yarns. Invite people to hold the end of the yarn, and throw the balls to another. As a web of many colors forms, think about true compassion being based on equality and interconnectedness. The woven yarn becomes a metaphor for the web of cosmic fire that constitutes the work of Geo-Justice on the planet.

The way ahead

... a larger vision of the world and the destiny of humankind... a common mind and spirit, a common sense of values on which it can agree and corporately act... a spirituality which can animate, develop, and strengthen the sense of being one human family with shared resources and mutual love for each other.[76]
—*Ursula King*

Towards transformation

In the pages of this book, I have talked about identifying our joy and our pain with the beauty and pain of the Earth. Personal pain when transformed into cosmic pain compels us into healing action. When we reflect on our engagement in Geo-Justice, we discover a cosmic ache as the channel for our work. In our vulnerability, we see that what we most want for our lives is possibility and hope. Our pain, both personal and planetary, animates us to reach for those possibilities. Therein resides the passion and potential of Geo-Justice and ourselves, a passion that arises from the interconnectedness of the psyche, society, global and local action, prophetic mysticism, and the Earth.

Deeply connecting to the Earth, we become flooded with a fertility and fruitfulness that overflows into all of life. We awaken as animators of a dream. Rooted in interconnectedness, we dare let go of whatever holds us back. We are united to an energy that animates our efforts in Geo-Justice.

The famous picture of the Earth taken from the depths of space shows our planet surrounded by an atmospheric envelope, a reminder of the numinous experiences that the Earth offers us. Our way ahead will be energized by our understanding of a new creation story that affirms our common experience of the Earth and the entire universe as a numinous, living, sentient creation. In this new relationship with the Earth, we move from exploitation to friendship and interdependence, from domination to ecological awareness. We come to see a scientific basis for seeing ourselves as "other"— we are not immune from what we do to others.

A renewed vision of the sacredness of *all* creation is born. Historic divisions of culture and geography will be transcended by a deep ecumenism born of our common connection to creation. We will be united by what we share in common—the earth, the seas, the sky.

From this perspective comes our context for action. In my experience, those who become aware of our common connection to creation begin to reflect on approaches to harmony and balance on the planet. Their actions are fueled by a value system that arises from both ancient wisdom and modern science.

As Elinor Gadon writes in *The Once and Future Goddess*, "Image is the key to transformation of our culture."[77] It is the image of the earth and our interconnectedness lies at the core of Geo-Justice. It is the image that gives birth to the new understanding, the new language, the new way of action.

In this process we go back to our roots. We retrieve our spiritual traditions and explore their implications for healing the Earth. This approach reveals to us the immanent presence of the divine in all of life. This awareness ignites imaginations; we feel excited about creating innovative programs for global alternatives and planetary peace.

We also are grateful for the present revelations of an emerging cosmology. It offers us a transformed world-view to assist in our work of healing. Oneness with the Earth will be characterized by profound trust, openness, and a willingness to implement the strategies that flow from this scientific perspective. Inclusiveness and participation on all levels will be reflected in our activities.

In our vision of a new global civilization, we will be true both to our destiny and to the needs of the Earth.

The cosmic invitation
The work of Geo-Justice invites us to our place on the planet.

That birthright has deep roots in our tradition. It challenges us to deepen our awareness of our oneness with the Earth. Such an awareness will encourage concrete regional efforts and alternative strategies of healing. The healing will be a microcosm of the new world order to come.

Within the deepest recesses of our being, each of us carries a spark. That spark is a microcosm of the energy of the cosmos. I could call this spark "soul" or "spirit," but "spark" conveys a less abstract picture. That spark is always new—it can erupt into flame unexpectedly. It is a reservoir of harmonious strength; it can fuel a relentless commitment. Like all fire, it is a source of energy. As a microcosm of the unfolding universe, it is always growing, always expanding, always in balance with the energy of the universe.

The work of Geo-Justice calls forth this spark in each of us. We are invited to an awakening awareness of the Earth and the cumulative events that move us inexorably toward the ongoing event of our day, a planetary Pentecost.

Within this context we can say:

- Each of us is invited to be participant and agent for weaving a tapestry of Geo-Justice, to be designer and architect of a mandala for the Earth, to be an instrument of harmony and balance for our planet.
- Each of us is invited to unity and oneness within ourselves, an adventure in global mysticism and peace.
- Each of us is invited to celebrate deeply the epiphanies of creation, discerned in the trajectory of each life.
- Each of us is invited to discover within ourselves what most ignites our psyche and connects us most profoundly to the journey of the cosmos.
- Each of us is invited to be a recipient of Geo-Justice in our own lives.
- Each of us is invited to co-create a planetary Pentecost for our time.

A doorway to destiny

Geo-Justice provides a window for the world. It is also a doorway for making a cosmic contribution. Doorways open, like opportunities. At this transformational moment, we have a marvelous opportunity. No previous generation has ever had such an opportunity—in part because no previous generation has ever faced such a planetary crisis. Few people even now understand the story of the earth and their place within it.

We are called to be open to the creativity and awesomeness of this moment, to celebrate it, savoring what is healing and mystical. We acknowledge that our invitation is to be a member of a team, convinced that nothing new will happen on our own. To respond fruitfully at this moment is to celebrate our connection to an ever-increasing community of all beings.

For we do not act alone. Rather, in responding to this invitation, we celebrate a growing conviction that the universe is acting through us. We are participants in a wondrous cosmic ritual.

The most important and psychically powerful events are often unplanned and full of surprise. What Jung called synchronicity, theology calls Resurrection. This dance toward the unplanned moment that we cannot force, but can only remain open to, is focused by silence, meditation, and a grateful celebration of our oneness with the Earth. Remembering these mutually magnetic moments, whenever they occur, will provide direction. Our energies and focus become aligned with the energy of the cosmos; we recognize a divine invitation to our place and path on the planet.

The passage toward Pentecost transforms us into people of protest, healing and wholeness. We protest the injustices, the wounds of the Earth, the "ism's" of our culture. We weave an interconnected web of life. We fashion avenues of communication and support; we re-vision justice-making. We work from a context of relationship and support; we re-create our vision and transform the context of our lives. Periodically we gather to share, to celebrate and be grateful, to energize our ongoing journeys.

We become increasingly aware of participating in a huge global event that is transforming society and ourselves.

There is in each of us an emerging power. It is within us, and we give it birth. We are simultaneously mothers, midwives, and children. We help a new order to be born; we are pregnant with the hope of a new era; we are ourselves being born to new life.

This dialectic invites us simultaneously to dive into our roots and soar into the new millennium. We stand at the doorway of a planetary Pentecost, an ongoing global event of peace that we simultaneously celebrate and create.

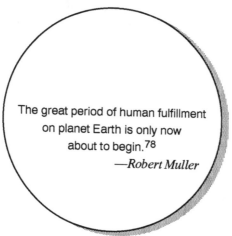

The great period of human fulfillment on planet Earth is only now about to begin.[78]

—*Robert Muller*

The quest for Geo-Justice

What is it that will evoke a vision, increase awareness, generate hope, and provide an energizing focus for our future? What can be the new soul of our Earth community, the energizing and organizing principle of our day?

We live in a time that more and more affirms the reality that history is upon us, that now is the time to realize our vision. Reading the signs of the times reveals the divine action in our day. The future will be born from envisioning the planet in new ways: of being, of relating, of dreaming, of building community, of nurturing our spiritual vision, of questing for our collective soul.

There will be other signs as well to assure us that we are on the right path. As our civilization enters a new era, and Geo-Justice moves from our psyches to the structures of our land, we will see a collective vision emerging. Out of that vision, our imaginations, memories, and dreams will find expression in concrete actions. The vision will include many elements,

- Prophecy. The call will emerge from both ecstasy and pain, and will generate hope for the future.

121

- Energy. Within the Earth reside resources of energy and transformation that can surface through our work.
- Education. We are moving beyond the violence of "banking" information, of domination of nature, and of conformity with the status quo, to critical reflection on reality in order to transform it.
- Psychology. Therapists and counselors are moving beyond an introspective preoccupation with human misery toward spiritual emergence and destiny.
- Movement and transformation. The new global society will be a non-organization, where people are informed, supported and empowered with others in common action.
- Creation. The invitation to Geo-Justice involves creating new lifestyles, and celebrating the beauty of the Earth.
- Compassionate minority. This minority is a sign of hope, a prophetic contradiction to the dominant culture, and a resource for whatever needs to be done to build a future filled with promise and hope.

Throughout the ages, [people have] longingly looked up to the harmony and order of the starry universe and have attuned [their] heartbeats to its measured movement.[79]
—*David Steindl-Rast*

A sheaf of spiritual practices

Our story is about woundedness and strength; our future lies in our contribution to the Earth. As we dissolve the dualism of psyche and society, the personal and political both become the context for connecting our experience to the larger cultural moment.

There is no blueprint for constructing Geo-Justice, as one might put together a child's wagon. However, I am convinced that a collective vision of Geo-Justice is indeed emerging from our cultural crises, from the beauty and pain of the Earth. We are being invited to discover and articulate that vision.

Breaking out of predictability, we engage in a dialogue with all creation. The dialogue has both beauty and pain as teacher, and celebration as reward. We pursue an Earth-centered approach to compassion. We integrate theology and experience, relationships and spirituality, roots and innovation, lifestyle and conviction.

In this dialogue, we remain open to questions and to surprise. We affirm that we are more than our brokenness. We acknowledge the deep wisdom that is nourished by silence, fueled by moral outrage and energized by a profound trust in life's unfolding. Moving toward both autonomy and interconnectedness, we experience a self-direction that demonstrates hope and trust in our inner voice, leading us into a future yet unborn. This self-direction finds its basis in the land, its vision in an unfolding future, and its energy in the moment we are about to live.

> By awakening our inner consciousness... through dream, myth, symbol, prayer, meditation, or other altered states of consciousness—that's where we're going to find the energy and insight and psychic strength...[80]
> —*Miriam Theresa MacGillis*

There are some specific things we can do to put together a framework of practices to animate our work of Geo-Justice. These practices are usually built around certain common elements:
- Music/gathering

- Humor
- Shared meal of food or drink
- Symbols from creation
- Bodily expression and movement
- Silence
- Sources from our tradition
- Moments for reflection/sending forth

For example, here are some things you could do that I, or members of my classes or workshops, have done.

- Spend 15 minutes a day reading the primary scripture of the cosmos by spending time in creation.
- Spend time with children and animals.
- Experience deeply and ritualize each of the seasons.
- Savor and celebrate the four elements in your life: earth, air, fire and water.
- Gratefully bless your food and remember the Earth as its source.
- Draw a map of your magnetic intuitions, your reciprocal attractions, where you have been, what is summoning you to life.
- Reflect on your experience and compose a "litany for the planet" by naming what needs to be born and what needs to die.
- Visualize Meister Eckhart's statement, "When I was born, all creation stood up and shouted, 'There is God'."[81]
- Develop art-full living through painting, clay, food, music and events of the day.
- Energize relationships of equity through storytelling, listening, ritual, and celebration.
- Explore in groups the divine language of dreams.
- Practise relinquishing your desire to control, compete, and center the world around yourself, in order to contribute more fully to the birth of the Earth in our time.
- Practise Thomas Berry's commandments of creation:
  "You shall remove all poison from the air."
  "You shall cease all pollution of the water."
  "You shall be open to the life-giving radiance of the sun."

"You shall support the self-sustaining forces of the universe."[82]

I invite you to add your own practices to these suggestions. In this way, we respond to the goal of life—soul-making and transformation.

Remember the counsel of Meister Eckhart, that after breakthrough, "We may return to the stable."[83] His words remind us that the deepest transformations in our lives are not necessarily accompanied by external manifestations. The return to the stable, the reentering of involvement in daily life, can also be an affirmation that our "breakthrough" was an authentic spiritual experience. The most authentic expression of Geo-Justice lies in who we are, not in what we do.

Process Reflection

1. Brainstorm on what attracts you to Geo-Justice. What do you most deeply believe about Geo-Justice? What contributions do you think you might make to Geo-Justice?
2. Choose the contributions that most appeal to you. Develop priorities and strategies. Try to identify some long-term strategies, and some that you can implement almost immediately.
3. From the many possibilities that emerge, decide what is most important. Make a commitment to do it.

The impulse for transformation

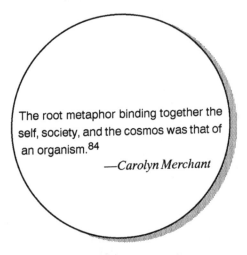

The root metaphor binding together the self, society, and the cosmos was that of an organism.[84]

—*Carolyn Merchant*

A primary goal of life is to discover our place, our role. We want to fulfill our potential; we want to make a significant contribution to life on this planet. This is usually best accomplished by living out what we *feel*, rather than what we *think*. Our minds can be easily misled by argument; our instincts are rarely swayed by rationalizations.

When we explore the patterns of the past, we usually find that our lives have not proceeded linearly like train tracks. A friend used to tell me: "Don't follow someone's path. Go your own way and leave a trail." When we listen to and act on our deepest feelings, we are "putting down our own tracks," creating our own futures, declaring that our lives are in our own hands. We are not trapped into conformity; our values are not limited to survival and domination where we always have to be right and others wrong.

Archimedes illustrated this capacity to create our own future: "Give me a place to stand and a lever long enough and I will move the world," he said. Each of us, from wherever we stand, can contribute our energy toward the transformation of the planet. This is justice-making, the fulfillment of our destiny.

If we are truly to move toward transformation, we will be in touch with our dreams and connected to our visions. Dreams retrieve from the unconscious the energetic and archetypal sources of our lives which have both global and personal significance. Visions help us to sketch, as it were, the painting that has not yet been put on canvas. They reveal options and possibilities; they animate practical action. They provide revelatory moments. Dreams and visions are the internal events, activities and indicators that point us towards our participation in the life of our planet.

If emotional turbulence results from this new involvement, we can best handle it by allowing it to surface, to be experienced. We continue to focus energy on the task at hand, the work of transformation; we see the emotional experience as fuel for our work.

Making decisions

Choices about participation in Geo-Justice will often uncover deep emotional pain. Often, what draws us into Geo-Justice is the connection between our own pain and that of the Earth. The choice to pursue a particular role in Geo-Justice can often touch deep-seated wounds. Rather than repress these feelings, we let them surface. The cleansing of our own emotional toxins opens the way to new insights and expression, and to a profound appreciation of beauty.

Choices, however, do have to be made. When Geo-Justice becomes our Window for the World, we may have to relinquish some associations with familiar places, people and tasks. Often, relationships are yet to be established; the nature of our work will be discovered as we explore it.

Relationships are a key factor in Geo-Justice. Our dominant culture typically pits relationships against self-direction. It suggests that we should not let friendships hold us back from our ambition. Geo-Justice does not pose such a dilemma.

We understand that all relationships are open to evolution and change. The development of intimacy need not create conflicting loyalties. Rather, each relationship is an opportunity to resolve emotional pressure and to renew our commitment, to each other, to a cause, and to the cosmos.

I use the term "intuitive magnetism" to describe attractions that are mutual, and that grow so strong they will not yield to fear, to argument, or to precedent. But we have not historically trusted that intuition. Although it is there, it may be embryonic. Premature attempts to make decisions intuitively may distort the direction implied by the choice. It is better to wait, until the intuition grows and becomes irresistible.

Pragmatic assessment of our present situation contributes to wisdom in making choices. We need to maximize the options that lie before us. In searching for and finding our place in Geo-Justice, it helps to observe the sequence of events preceding a particular moment. Too often, we become preoccupied too quickly with issues and questions. By simply observing, we may discover that preceding events and the current context both show us moving in a particular direction. This recognition reduces the possibility of circular thinking, of going round and round without direction or resolution. Non-judgmental assessment of options also avoids those self-deprecating attacks of guilt and doubt that render decision-making so difficult. A pragmatic approach to the here and now helps move us into the next phase of our work.

Remember always that who we are takes precedence over what we do. The deepest transformations in our lives, the most significant shifts, can and do take place regardless of circumstances. In that sense, our lives are not circumstantially circumscribed; we change the world by being changed ourselves. Our work in Geo-Justice starts by discovering who we are and taking full responsibility for where we are in our journey.

Now I see the secret of the making of the best persons. It is to grow in the open air, and to eat and sleep with the Earth.[85]
—*Walt Whitman*

The time is now...

Although it's not possible to see into the future, we do have to make decisions. Under the constraints of schedules, time frames, and personal commitments, a choice presents itself. Fear and indecision are predictable, but the decision will be made. Friends and confidants can be helpful and supportive at this time; but the decision remains our own.

We need to draw on as many vehicles as possible for gaining insight into our lives. No source of knowledge is out of bounds, no access to mystery and the sacred need escape us. Somatic therapy, parapsychology, meditative techniques—all offer routes for exploring significant events in our lives that are not available by more traditional, empirical means. However, we should never relinquish responsibility for our life choices to these methods of exploring self-understanding and our future. Neither psychology nor scripture, tarot nor tradition, reading our palms or reading the stars, can provide answers for us. We are responsible for discovering our own calling, for living our own life, for choosing our own place in the work of Geo-Justice.

Our work is to bring harmony, balance and peace to the planet. Whatever the focus of individual work, the most important dimension is that we see our efforts within a larger context of interconnected energies acting as one huge transformer, illuminating and awakening the entire Earth. This is the planetary Pentecost.

As we contemplate our future, we realize that a new moment is upon us. We stand on the threshold of a new beginning. The doorway of opportunity opens into the third millennium.

This doorway of opportunity challenges us to be workers for a planetary Pentecost, to animate the energy necessary to move us into the third millennium. A Paschal moment of death and rebirth summons us. To what?

To a time of future, filled with promise, rising from a
  dangerous past.

To a time of hope, rising from despair.

To a time of mystery, rising from a fixed and frozen now.

To a time of participation, rising from a passive observation
  of life.

To a time of adventurous self-understanding, rising from an

armored resistance.

To a time of global concern for our endangered Earth, rising from a time of privatized domination.

To a time of integration and tenderness toward the Earth, rising from extinction, waste and planetary poison.

To a time of global consciousness, rising from our fragmented psyches.

To a time for Geo-Justice, rising from the resources and legacies of those who have gone before.

High Perches/Low Aspirations
Isolated people
Sitting on high stools
Seemingly espousing
Low aspirations
For their lives.
Gazing into a silver tube
Belching out the venom
Of a failed leadership
Of a previously promised land
From these high perches
Unreflected awareness
Seems to ooze from somewhere
And spill into an ever darkening room.

—Conlon

It is precisely within this context of "isolated people… in an ever darkening room" that Geo-Justice is needed and makes sense. Those who have labored long to build the Earth are being discovered; others are awakening to the need; much that is hopeful is happening. Within the collective unconscious of the culture evolves an awareness that our primary concern is the Earth. We are moving toward a turning point, a convergence of awareness and action. We are here to heal the planet.

Geo-Justice puts us in touch with the barriers that hold us back, that divert us from our path. Convinced of the preciousness of all creation, we are flooded with profound gratitude. More and more we see life as an unlimited possibility in a unifying context, a possibility that offers a new sense of hope, future, and an integration of diverse energies. As someone said:

"If you can imagine it, you can achieve it.

If you can dream it, you can become it."

Discovering moments of cosmic wisdom

Geo-Justice invites us to become open to cosmic energies in our life and work. We have an experience of being drawn by powerful yet open-ended forces. The irresistibility of this invitation is a sign of the power of these forces within us. These forces push us to risk moving beyond the definable guidelines of career, to an experience that is undefinable but inevitable, constant but constantly changing, always unfinished but complete in itself.

Access to this fuller and deeper way of living is nourished and focused by moments of reflection and aloneness. Often these moments provide the opportunity to respond to an invitation of some "other"—be it a person, an idea, a plant or an animal. The propensity to fall in love, to expand our horizons, to achieve a sense of wholeness—all these increase our awareness.

We become acutely aware of the dialectic in interdependence. The moment-by-moment choices we make preclude any sets of presuppositions and guidelines. We are on own own. At the same time, we are also supported by the emerging consensus of an expanding global community. We are independent and autonomous; yet we are interdependent and part of a vast movement taking place around the world. Our awareness of this dialectic generates solidarity and purpose, dissolves despair, and supports courage in listening to our inner voice as we pursue unpredictable paths.

Knowing our place in the cosmos is a lifelong and continuous process. It deepens, expands and is constantly accompanied by unknowing and uncertainty. In accessing the unknown, we search for a more profound source from which to live.

At the same time, the energy of the cosmos provides opportunity to awaken to the deep significance of our own journeys. Our interest and passion are as fragile as our endangered planet—yet like butterflies flashing with color in an afternoon garden, every one matters and contributes to the beauty of the whole.

In this journey of faith, we discover the palpable presence of the divine. A growing global awareness anchors us in the cosmos. The divine presence awakens primordial energies in our bodies, and we feel ourselves connected with all of creation. Our prophetic contribution to the universe captivates and enchants us. Cosmic wisdom unfolds life's surprises—our privilege is to be open to the moment of the unexpected.

The Word of God is always, "In the beginning." And this means that it is always in the process of being born, and is always already born.[86]

—*Meister Eckhart*

Giving birth to our future

We can no longer respond effectively to the problems of the Earth from the standpoint of the sovereignty of any one nation or group of nations. Because our experience is rooted in the beauty and pain of the Earth, it contains a deep sense of protest, a commitment to prophecy which demands concrete action. Fresh energy, released from the connection of the psyche and society, results in new frameworks and forms, new ways of seeing the world that influence the work of global transformation.

The challenges of the future are many. The concerns of women, ecological devastation, AIDS, the extinction of species, drug abuse, the desperation of our cities, the fate of the poor, the greenhouse effect, the translation of ideals into social programs, the rape of the rain forests, world hunger—all of these demand our attention.

Geo-Justice, more broadly grasped, offers a new language, a new approach, which seeks to put all these problems into a single unified context for protecting the planet and transforming human culture. In Geo-Justice, through working on any one of these problems, we work on them all.

There is a profound connection between our personal journeys and the great issues of our time.

We are all called to the work of Geo-Justice; within this work, we provide the support and the resources for those who are just coming to a realization of their task. We discover where good things are happening, and strive to make them better. We multiply the consensus by coordinating the efforts of others. As we move from action to reflection, from reflection to imagination, from imagination to integration, we celebrate a new world being born.

There is profound goodness in life. The goodness shows up in the banquet of beauty that surrounds us. The rich cultural diversity of the peoples of the Earth is itself a banquet. So is the gentle strength of prophets who give voice to the voiceless, roofs to the homeless, and hospitality to all who would join an ever-increasing circle of hope.

Celebrating that goodness, we work to dissolve the institutionalized violence expressed in racism and other "'ism's." We honor our ancestors, upon whose shoulders we stand. We acknowledge ancient wisdom. We find the newness of the divine child in each beginning, and tenderness and compassion as the crescendo and culmination of life. History's unfolding provides us with an evolutionary consciousness. Memories remind us of those times when community action was shut down and political paranoia flourished in the culture. But from this phoenix came new beginnings. The resistance of political and economic structures, and the inflexibility of established modes of thinking, generated their own friction. In response, people turned within for healing, and to each other for support. At that critical moment, newness was born. New metaphors and symbols for peace tumbled into consciousness.

> Humanity could be on the threshold of an evolutionary leap.[87]
> —Peter Russell

That process continues today. It is not just continuing, but getting stronger. Matter comes alive; the Earth becomes our sacred place of origin; renewal and restoration span the globe. We are the

Earth, and we are called to heal the planet. A planetary shift, a homecoming, has taken place.

From an age of homelessness, we come home to ourselves and to the Earth.

From being cut off from our origins, we reclaim our creation story.

From being wounded, we acknowledge our strength.

From being empty, we become full.

From being destructive, we are healed.

From being dominated, we are receptive.

From being alone, we are at one.

From being driven to chaos, we are at peace.

From being lost, we are found.

From being frightened, we are focused.

From being passengers on an endangered spaceship Earth, we are drawn together to take command of our common course of survival.

From the precipice of doubt, we become fully engaged in life.

—*Conlon*

The birth of the planet

The future is more beautiful than all the pasts.[88]

—*Teilhard de Chardin*

More and more people are thinking about their vocational destiny. A woman from New York and a young man from New Hampshire recently spoke to me, with similar questions and experiences. They'd been to the Third World, they'd worked with the poor, they'd been involved with justice for years, and they still wondered what they were called to do with their lives.

As we approach the new era that awaits us, I believe that voices like theirs represent many, many more people. These people long to participate creatively in the birth of the planet. For this birth, we are all midwives, and we are all at the same time birthing ourselves.

A prerequisite of this collective awareness is a deep letting go and emptying. This letting go and emptying cleanses us. It frees us to contact both the pain of the Earth and the deepest joy of our lives. When we know that we are living out our deepest destiny and calling, we will experience a flood of creativity to heal the Earth.

In all this, we realize the wisdom of envisioning the Earth as the operative myth for our times. In fact, as I have proposed, Geo-Justice suggests a preferential option for the Earth as the perspective for our work.

135

This operative myth is sorely needed for our culture. We have been taught, as Frederick Turner points out in his book, *Beyond Geography*, to repress the wilderness within and consequently oppress the wilderness without. He writes: "The coming of European civilization is the story of a civilization that substituted history for myth."[89] He argues that this repression of the wilderness in our psyche has caused our culture to project and legitimize war, savagery, genocide and ecocide. By contrast, the Dene people of Canada's North West Territories state: "We have no word that means wilderness, as anywhere we go is our home. It doesn't make sense to destroy our home."[90]

As we search for our place in giving birth to the planet through the work of Geo-Justice, we recognize the importance of the recovery of the myth that Frederick Turner calls the "symbolic, instinctual response of the organism of life; an expressive language of life."[88]

A response to crises

The focus of our lives is to live in harmony with the universe. A crisis occurs when we experience discord between the direction of our lives and the cosmic truth of who we are. This crisis may appear as the disruption of a relationship or a career, excessive fear, doubt, defensiveness, or physical illness. All of these may be a divine reminder that we are straying from our true destiny. Our disease is an attempt of the cosmos to bring change into our lives and into the universe.

Properly understood, a crisis becomes an opportunity. We have a fresh chance to realign our lives with our true vocation and purpose. This change is like altering a sailboat's course to compensate for a changing wind.

Redirecting our lives brings great joy, but is often accompanied by deep pain. Any change involves breaking down ingrained patterns of thought and living and creating new ones. Meister Eckhart's counsel that we must let go in order to re-enter is apt. But despite the pain of change, the subsequent shift makes it increasingly possible to savor life's greatest gifts and achieve harmony in our lives. We become an expression of the Geo-Justice that we are invited to create.

Many people today are experiencing personal crises. These crises, in many ways, parallel the planetary earthquake this is upon us. They are reminders that the divine energy of the universe sometimes calls us to change our patterns of living and being. Living in harmony with our vocational destiny involves a breakdown of old structures and ways of living. To be fully and truly our real selves involves a life of adventure and unending change. We trust the apparent crises in our lives as opportunities for healing, learning and deepening an awareness of our destiny.

Otto Rank, the prophetic psychiatrist, claims that as each civilization comes to an end and a new culture is about to be born, the quest for a new soul becomes a common pursuit.[92] What is to be the new soul for our culture? I believe the new soul for our time is a new type of human being. We are called to trust the preferential option for the Earth as the vehicle for our growth and for the health of all creation.

One of the most joyful experiences of life is to know that we are following our deepest purpose, fascination, intention and call. As we move from apparent meaningless to a meaningful life, joy happens. Carl Jung articulated our desire for a meaningful vocation when he wrote: "True personality always has vocation: an irrational factor that fatefully forces a person to emancipate himself [or herself] from the herd of its trodden paths."[93] Vocation is a confidence that life is going somewhere worthwhile.

From complexity to synthesis

Another great thinker, Teilhard de Chardin, saw the pursuit of vocational destiny through the lens of evolution. He identified the evolutionary process in both cosmos and culture as a movement from complexity to synthesis. This description fits well the process of seeking our destinal vocation. We are drawn toward our true destiny like iron filings toward a magnet. This attraction pulls us toward the work that most deeply fascinates us, and also toward others with whom we share similar magnetic intuitions.

Destiny and vocation together become an evolutionary impulse for transformation. We know we are needed; we have a purpose. Having found this vantage point, we feel most alive. This discovery of our destiny is like smaller flames being drawn together into larger flames. It is like discovering a common attraction that draws apparently scattered elements together to unite them. This process shows up socially when individuals cluster together to form a new social organism.

Our approach will be much like a mating, a hunger for mystical communion. This process has a mysterious sense of attraction. As we unite our flames of expectation with others who share the awareness that we are all one, we find we are all connected. Together we move forward and become one. This event is an expression of the divine Spirit, a planetary Pentecost—a response to an inner call to be truly who we are. It fulfills our deepest dream, to experience ourselves as truly connected to the whole—connected to God, to nature, to others, and to self.

Once we become aware of this deep attraction, no force can keep us apart. We are conscious of participating in an ever-increasing critical mass of purposefulness. Dormant powers awaken to their fullest capacity.

Each of us has a portion of the wisdom necessary to accomplish this great task. Collectively, we become architects and co-creators, birthing a new civilization, integrating the planet into a harmonious living body.

To live our destiny and vocation, then, is to experience a sense of oneness with others who share a common call. It is also to discover our place: a place of homecoming, of healing woundedness, of spiritual awakening. As people discover and live intentionally their vocational destiny, they in turn discover each other. They will weave together an organic tapestry of relationships that transform people in a transformed world.

And each creature contributes to the whole, to the web that sustains all life in ways that we are only beginning to discover.[94]

—Jane Blewett

Archetypes of a new humanity

At this moment, we stand at the threshold of a radical transformation on the planet. In our common journey, each of us has a unique contribution to make. Each person possesses a dimension of the unfolding pattern of the universe. Each has a part in this great cosmic drama. Each of us is an agent of transformation, animating the new millennium.

The new civilization that emerges from this process will be organic, renewable and self-organizing. This movement from complexity to synthesis will continually increase a sense of purpose and freedom. A common vision leads to a recognition of the oneness of all creation. As our planet integrates into one body, we come to the incarnation of a new humanity, a new creation.

The event of the planetary Pentecost, the fulfillment of our deepest longing for communion, will be ours when the Earth gives birth to itself as one. This healing of all separation will happen when more and more people enter into resonance with each other and with the planet. Within this energy field, creativity will blossom, and our gifts will be acknowledged. A new Earth will be born.

Patience, compassion and understanding will guide the process. With deep reverence and purpose, we will live our lives in trust, cooperation, and resonance. In this context, new social configurations and processes move us toward the birth of the new creation.

Because the destruction of the biosphere has replaced nuclear war as the major threat to human survival, we focus on the transformation of ecological devastation and negative patterns of living. We set out to weave together a fabric of kindness and a tapestry of peace, for ourselves and for the planet.

We know that peace is possible when we live from the perspective of a preferential option for the Earth. We acknowledge everything we receive as a gift. We celebrate the Earth as the unifying myth of our time. The birth of our planet as a living body is the primary impulse for our time. Through it, the energy of the universe is available for transformation, as the old order gives way to a new world order about to be born.

This is the adventure of Geo-Justice. It invites us onward.

139

A canticle for Geo-Justice

Where there are ruptures in creation,
We are aroused to peace.

Where there is disquietude,
We are invited to balance.

Where there is discord,
We are attuned to resonance.

In and through the pain of our wounded planet,
We are called to make our Easter with the Earth.

From collapse and devastation
We rediscover within the risen heart of the universe
    Cosmic peace
    Profound harmony
    Deep balance
    Compassionate resonance
    Pentecost for the Earth and
    Geo-Justice with the universe.

—Conlon

Process reflection
1. Present a guided meditation where participants are invited to identify with one of four types of creatures:
   a) winged (relating to air)
   b) fish (relating to water)
   c) four-legged (relating to the earth)
   d) mythological (relating to fire).
2. Invite participants to reflect on their experiences in the light of one of these four groups.
3. After the guided meditation, the people gather in one of the four groups and design a dramatized response to their destiny, as they see it in relation to the group they have chosen.
4. Their dramatizations are presented.

5. The participants are invited to reflect on their destinal vocations in light of this experience:

    a) their dream about the future they would like to create,

    b) through listening, challenge others and themselves to actualize gifts in developing a focus for the future.

6. While gentle environmental music plays, move around the room and extend a silent greeting to other people in the room.

Appendices

Projects and people

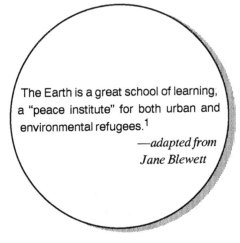

The Earth is a great school of learning, a "peace institute" for both urban and environmental refugees.[1]

—adapted from
Jane Blewett

I have listed below (in alphabetical order) persons and programs whom I know to be particularly attuned to the work of Geo-Justice.

Regional Connectors for Base
  Groups in Creation Spirituality
Mary Ann Quinn,
110 West Grant St., #15B,
Minneapolis, MN 55403

Brooklyn Ecumenical Cooperatives
Richard Harmon
541 Atlantic Ave.
Brooklyn, NY 11217

Center for Ecology and Spirituality
Port Burwell, Ontario, Canada
NOJ 1TO

Campaign for the Earth
David Gershon,
449A Route 28A
West Hurley, NY 12491

Center for Studies in Science and
  Spirituality
Brian Swimme
753 Ashbury Street
San Francisco, CA 94117

Earth Stewards Network
Danann Perry and Diana Glasgow
P.O. Box 10697
Winslow, WA 98110

Jack Egan
Office of Community Affairs
DePaul University
243 S. Wabash
Chicago, IL 60604

Paulo Freire
Minister for Education,
Valenca 170, Sumare
Sao Paulo, Brazil 626270

Global Education Associates
Jerry and Patricia Mische
Suite 456
Inter Church Center
475 Riverdale Drive
New York, NY 10115

The Institute for Contextual
    Theology
Albert Nolan
Johannesburg, South Africa

Institute in Culture and Creation
    Spirituality
Matthew Fox
Holy Names College
3500 Mountain Blvd.
Oakland, CA 94619

Instituto Bartolome de las Casas
Gustavo Gutierrez
Casilla 3234
Limo 100, Peru

Office for Human Development
Desmond De Sousa
Dona Matilde Bldg., No. 301
876G Apacible
P.O. Box EA-12
Ermita, Manila, Philippines

The Riverdale Center
    for Religious Research
Thomas Berry
5801 Palisade Ave.
Bronx, NY 10471

Spiritual Emergence Network
1010 Doyle Street
Suite 10
Menlo Park, CA 94025

Holotropic Breathwork
Stan and Christina Grof/Jeneane
Prevatt
20 Sunny Side
Suite A, #253
Mill Valley, CA 94941

University for Peace
Robert Muller
P.O. Box 199-1250
Escazu, Costa Rica

Worldwatch Institute
Lester Brown
1776 Massachusetts Ave. NW
Washington, DC 20006

[1]Jane Blewett "Social Justice and Creation Spirituality," *The Way*, (January 1989)

Center for the Third Millennium

A generic proposal that contains the components necessary for the work of Geo-Justice, intended as a focus for the work of Geo-Justice in our time.

1. The Context

Each cultural moment reveals the appropriate action responses for that time. As we stand on the threshold of the 21st century, we ask: What needs to be done to bring about the new millennium? What are the educational resources, projects and praxis that will provide information and support to catalyze and deepen the unfolding of this time?

2. The Cultural Moment

Reflection on the unfolding of past events instructs us that each period in history provides its own unique approaches to change and transformation. In recent years we have witnessed the growth of the human potential movement, depth and transpersonal psychology, community organization and development of a Geo-Justice theology from the perspectives of liberation and creation, a spiritual awakening in the culture and the revisioning of a new origin story for ourselves and the planet. Within these developments resides the resources and wisdom for what lies ahead. The proposal for a Center for the Third Millennium is intended as a resource for the moment that awaits us.

3. Components of the Project

The Center for the Third Millennium will consist of these components:
  a) Research and development: The Center will focus on the preparation of monographs, manuscripts and periodicals to articulate and focus the cultural resources for our day.
  b) Education: The Center will provide a context in which to

reflect critically on the work of cultural therapy. Drawing on a faculty with a broad-based perspective on the new cosmology, the curriculum will focus on issues relating to: the new cosmology, global issues, community organization, popular education, consciousness research and transpersonal psychology, the spirituality of the Earth, a theology of Geo-Justice, and cultural projects and personal paths designed for global harmony and Geo-Justice.

c) Staff: A small staff for coordination and support will focus on the research and educational process. Staff will be accompanied by an adjunct faculty grounded in the areas mentioned above.

d) Curriculum development: The Center proposes a curriculum focused on: cosmology, global issues, community, theology, psychology, spirituality and education catalyzed by processes of in-depth self-exploration to enable participants to focus more fully on their place and path. Additional areas for reflection will be generated by the participants.

4. Projects and praxis

Through critical reflection on past experience and current engagements, participants will envision their contribution to the culture and future areas of concern.

5. Interns and recall

Participants will be encouraged to utilize their back-home situation as a continuation of the learning process. Subsequently a recall session will review their engagement and plan future work.

6. Written and recorded resources

The Center will make shareable the wisdom that emerges from the praxis of its participants through written and recorded resources.

7. Information and support

The Center will set as a priority strategies for continuing information and support for graduates and associates. This will be accomplished through written and oral communication, periodic gatherings, and shared reflections generated from their praxis.

8. Implementation

A coordinator will establish an office and focus on the following:

- formation of a birthing committee
- location and institutional connections
- publicity and time frame for implementing various phases
- fund-raising
- affiliation with like-minded groups
- mailing lists and target constituencies
- composition and promulgation of a Center "position statement"

9. Concluding remarks

A synthesis of the best of cultural work, a spirituality of the Earth and the wisdom of the new cosmology has much to offer the onset of the 21st century. The Center for the Third Millennium is designed as a resource and research center for this important moment in history: a place to gather, mine the resources of the culture and explore their particular contribution for our future.

Endnotes

The earth story for our time

1 Sean McDonagh, *To Care For The Earth: A Call to a New Theology*, (Santa Fe, New Mexico: Bear & Company, 1985) p. 119.

2 René Dubois, *A God Within*, (New York: Charles Scribner & Sons, 1972) p. 294.

3 quoted in Charles M. Johnston, *The Creative Imperative*, (Berkeley, CA: Celestial Arts, 1980) p. 47

4 Class notes from a program on Community Education and Development, at the University of Toronto, 1976.

The vision of Geo-Justice

5 quoted in Margo Adair, "Imagine a World..." between the lines, Vol. 1, No. 1, 1989

6 "Ecological Kristallnacht," March 19, 1989, p. 27.

7 Thomas Berry, *The Riverdale Papers*, (unpublished monograph).

8 *Great Spirit, Great Nation*, from the presentation at the Institute for Christian Life in Canada for Fr. Rene Fumoleau, August 1977.

9 Robinson Jeffers, "The Answer" from *The Earth Speaks*, (Warrenville, IL.: The Institute for Earth Education, 1983), p. 136.

10 René Dubois, *A God Within*, p. 294.

A new soul for justice-making

11 José and Miriam Argüelles, *Mandala*, (Boston and London: Shambhala, 1985), p. 12.

12 *Ibid.*

13 Carl Jung, *Man and His Symbols*, (Garden City, NY: Doubleday & Co., 1964), p. 225.

14 Argüelles, *Mandala*, p. 12.

15 Matthew Fox, *Meditations With Meister Eckhart*, (Santa Fe: Bear & Company, 1983), p. 12.

16 James H. Forest, *Thomas Merton: A Pictorial Biography*. (New York: Paulist Press, 1980), p. 69.

Peace with the Earth

17 *Tico Times*: Editorial (English Language Weekly), San Jose, Costa Rica. June 23, 1989.

18 "Seeking the True Meaning of Peace." Conference Facilitation Document. University of Peace. San Jose, Costa Rica. June 23-30, 1989. Page 3.

19 *Declaration of Human Responsibility for Peace and Sustainable Development*. Costa Rica: Government of Costa Rica, 1989.

20 From a lecture by Robert Muller at "Seeking the True Meaning of Peace" Conference, University of Peace. San Jose, Costa Rica. June 30, 1989.
21 "Planet of the Year: Endangered Earth," *Time* magazine, Jan. 2, 1989, p. 30.

Historical perspective
22 Compiled by James Larson and Madge Micheels-Cyrus, *Seeds of Peace*, (Philadelphia and Santa Cruz: New Society Publishers, 1987), p. 270.
23 Matthew Fox, *The Coming of the Cosmic Christ*, (San Francisco: Harper & Row, 1988), p. 34.

A planetary earthquake
24 Joe Holland, "The Post Modern Cultural Earthquake," Center for Concern, Washington, D.C., 1984.
25 Albert Nolan, *God in South Africa: The Challenge of the Gospel*, (Durban, South Africa: Wm. Eerdmans, 1988) p. 132.
26 Fox, *Meditations With Meister Eckhart*, p. 92.
27 quoted in Charles M. Johnston, *The Creative Imperative*, p. 349.

Signposts for Geo-Justice
28 Jane Blewett "Social Justice and Creation Spirituality," *The Way*, (London, January 1989), p. 13.
29 Thomas Merton, Seeds of Contemplation, (New York: Dell, 1953), p. 21.
30 Wendell Berry, "The Unforeseen Wilderness," from *The Earth Speaks*, (Warrenville, IL: Institute for Earth Education, 1983), p. 181.
31 Henri J. M. Nouwen, *The Wounded Healer*, (Garden City, NY: Doubleday, 1972), p. xvi.
32 Thomas Berry, *The Dream of the Earth*, (San Francisco: Sierra Club Books, 1988), p. 122.
33 Brian Swimme, "The Resurgence of Cosmic Storytellers," *The Way*, (London: January 1989), p. 36.
34 Thomas Berry, *The Dream of the Earth*, p. 5.
35 quoted in Charles M. Johnston, *The Creative Imperative*, p. 131.

The global component
36 Pierre Teilhard de Chardin, *Toward the Future*, (New York and London: Harcourt Brace Jovanovich, 1984), p. 199.
37 Matthew Fox, *Meditations With Meister Eckhart*, p. 22.
38 David Steindl-Rast, *Human Survival and Consciousness Evolution*, (Albany, State University of New York Press, 1988), p. 94.
39 Thomas Berry, *The Riverdale Papers* (unpublished monograph).
40 Pierre Teilhard de Chardin, *Building the Earth*, (New York: Avon, 1963) foreword.
41 Thomas Berry, *The Dream of the Earth*, p. 195.

The local component

[42] Saul D. Alinsky, *Reveille for Radicals*, (New York: Random House, 1969), p. viii.

[43] Gary Snyder, *Creation* magazine, March/April 1987, p. 8.

[44] Starhawk, *Truth or Dare*, (San Francisco: Harper & Row, 1987) p. 15.

[45] Albert Nolan, *God in South Africa*, p. 14.

[46] quoted in Irenie Diamond and Gloria Feman Orenstein, *Reweaving the World: The Emergence of Ecofeminism*, (San Francisco: Sierra Club Books, 1990) p. 59.

[47] Madonna Kolbenschlag, *Lost in the Land of Oz: The Search for Identity and Community in American Life*, (San Francisco, Harper & Row, 1988), p. 170.

[48] Saul D. Alinsky, (ICUIS #922, 1972), pp. 178-9.

The psycho-social component

[49] Paulo Freire, *Pedagogy of the Oppressed*, (New York: Seabury Press, 1970), p. 98.

[50] Robert N. Bellah, Richard Madsen, William M. Sullivan, Ann Swidler and Steven M. Tipton, *Habits of the Heart:Individualism and Commitment in American Life*, (New York: Harper & Row, 1985) pp. 290-1.

[51] Stanislav Grof, *Beyond the Brain*, (Albany: State University of New York Press, 1985) p. 92.

[52] Stanislav Grof, ed., *Ancient Wisdom and Modern Science*, (Albany: State University of New York Press, 1984), p. vii.

[53] Thomas Berry, "Finding Heaven on Earth," *New Age Journal*, (Boulder, CO) April 1990, p. 131.

[54] Stanislav Grof and Marjorie Livingston Valier, eds., *Human Survival and Consciousness Evaluation*, (Albany: State University of New York, 1988) p. 76.

[55] Stanislav Grof and Christina Grof, eds., *Spiritual Emergency*, (Los Angeles: Jeremy P. Tarcher Inc., 1989) p. 235.

Towards a theology of Geo-Justice

[56] Tissa Balasuriya, *Planetary Theology*, (Maryknoll, NY: Orbis Books, 1984), p. 15.

Healing the Earth

[57] Sean McDonagh, *To Care for the Earth*, p. 119.

[58] *Bible, New International Version* (Grand Rapids, MI: Zondervan Bible Publishers)

[59] Richard P. McBrien, *Catholicism*, (Minneapolis: Winston Press, 1981) p. 1058.

Practices in Geo-Justice

[60] Paulo Freire, Notes on "Seminar on Community Education and Development," (Toronto: Ontario Institute for Studies in Education, 1976), p. 5.

[61] Matthew Fox, *Illuminations of Hildegard of Bingen*, (Santa Fe, New

Mexico: Bear & Company, 1986). p. 19.
[62] Paulo Freire, *Pedagogy of the Oppressed*, p. 86.
[63] Notes of Generative Themes from a course on Ministry and Culture, Toronto, 1984.
[64] Parker J. Palmer, *The Chronicle of Higher Education*, (Washington, DC) February 23, 1990, page A3.
[65] Michael Czerny, S.J., and Jamie Swift, *Getting Started on Social Analysis in Canada*, (Toronto: Between The Lines, 1985), p. 14.
[66] Michael Czerny, S.J., and Jamie Swift, *Getting Started in Social Analysis in Canada*, p. 14.
[67] Paulo Freire, Notes, p. 11.
[68] Saul D. Alinsky, *Rules for Radicals*, (New York: Random House, 1971), pp. 58-9.
[69] Deborah Brandt and Carlos Friere (illustrator), *Naming the Moment: Political Analysis for Action, A Manual for Community Groups*, (Toronto: Jesuit Centre for Social Faith and Justice, 1989)
[70] Jane Blewett, "Social Justice and Creation Spirituality," *The Way*, (January 1989), pp. 14-15.

Exploring the mandala
[71] Stanislav Grof, *Beyond the Brain*, p. 391

A window for the world
[72] quoted in Michael Linfield, *The Dance of Change: An Eco-Spiritual Approach to Transformation*, (New York: Routledge & Kegan Paul, 1986) p. 146.
[73] Thomas Berry, "Finding Heaven on Earth," *New Age Journal* (Boulder, CO) April 1990, p. 139.
[74] Gregory Baum and Duncan Cameron, *Ethics and Economics: Canada's Catholic Bishops on the Economic Crisis*, (Toronto: James Lorimer & Company, 1984), p. 67.
[75] Jean Larson and Madge Micheels-Cyrus, *Seeds of Peace: A Catalogue of Quotations*, (Philadelphia and Santa Cruz: New Society Publishers, 1987), p. 249.

The way ahead
[76] Ursula King, *The Spirit of One Earth: Reflections on Teilhard de Chardin and Global Spirituality*, (New York: Paragon House, 1989), pp. 5-6.
[77] Elinor Gadon, *The Once and Future Goddess*, (San Francisco: Harper & Row, 1989) p. 370.
[78] Robert Muller, *New Genesis: Shaping a Global Spirituality*, (Garden City, New York: Doubleday, 1984) p. 8.
[79] David Steindl-Rast, *A Listening Heart: The Art of Contemplative Living*, (New York: Crossroad, 1983), p. 17.
[80] Miriam Theresa MacGillis, "Living the New Story," *In Context*, No. 24,

81 Winter 1990, p. 27.

82 Matthew Fox, *Meditations With Meister Eckhart*, p. 12.

83 Thomas Berry, public lecture, Oakland, Calif., 1985.

Fox, *Meditations With Meister Eckhart*, p. 91.

The impulse for transformation

84 Carolyn Merchant, *The Death of Nature*, (San Francisco: Harper & Row, 1980)

85 Walt Whitman, "Leaves of Grass", *The Earth Speaks*, (Warrenville, IL: Institute for Earth Education, 1983) p. 12.

86 Matthew Fox, *Meditations with Meister Eckhart*, p. 72.

87 Peter Russell, *The Global Brain: Speculations on the Evolutionary Leap to Planetary Consciousness*, (Los Angeles: Jeremy P. Tarcher Inc., 1983), p. 7.

The birth of the planet

88 Blanche Marie Gallagher, *Meditations with Teilhard de Chardin*, (Sante Fe: Bear & Co., 1988), p. 143.

89 Frederick Turner, *Beyond Geography: The Western Spirit Against the Wilderness*, (New Brunswick, NJ: Rutgers University Press, 1983) p. 10.

90 *Great Spirit, Great Nation*, from the presentation at the Institute for Christian Life in Canada for Fr. Rene Fumoleau, August 1977.

91 Frederick Turner, *Beyond Geography*, p. 10.

92 Quoted in Matthew Fox, "Searching for Authentically Human Images of Soul in Meister Eckhart and Teresa of Avila," *Current Trends in Spirituality Today*, Nov. 1985, p. 1-35.

93 Barbara Marx Hubbard, *The Hunger of Eve*, (Eastsound, Washington: Island Pacific NW, 1989), p. 42.

94 Jane Blewett "Social Justice and Creation Spirituality," *The Way*, (January 1989), pp. 15-16.

Bibliography

Resources in Geo-Justice

The following list is by no means an exhaustive survey of literature related to Geo-Justice. Any such survey would require some 20 pages of this book, or more. Rather, I have attempted to identify those books and resources most likely, in my view, to be helpful to readers interested in pursuing this subject further. Some of the sources indicated in the endnotes have not been included in this bibliography—I also commend them to interested readers.

Alinsky, Saul D. *Reveille for Radicals*. New York: Random House, 1969.
— *Rules for Radicals*. New York: Random House, 1971.

Argüelles, José, and Miriam Argüelles. *Mandala*. Boston and London: Shambhala, 1985.

Balasuriya, Tissa. *Planetary Theology*. Maryknoll, NY: Orbis Books, 1984.

Baum, Gregory. *Man Becoming: God in Secular Experience*. New York: Herder & Herder, 1970.
— *Religion and Alienation: A Theological Reading of Sociology*. New York, Paramus and Toronto: Paulist Press, 1976.
— *Compassion and Solidarity*. Toronto: CBC Enterprises, 1987.

Baum, Gregory, and Duncan Cameron. *Ethics and Economics: Canada's Catholic Bishops on the Economic Crisis*. Toronto: James Lorimer & Company, 1984.

Bellah, Robert N., Richard Madsen, William M. Sullivan, Ann Swidler, and Steven M. Tipton. *Habits of the Heart: Individualism and Commitment in American Life*. New York: Harper & Row, 1985.

Berry, Thomas. *The Dream of the Earth*. San Francisco: Sierra Club Books, 1988.
— *The Riverdale Papers*, unpublished monograph. Riverdale, NY: Riverdale Center for Religious Research.

Boff, Leonardo. *Ecclesiogenesis: The Base Communities Reinvent the Church*. Maryknoll, NY: Orbis Books, 1986.

Bohm, David, and F. David Peat. *Science, Order and Creativity: A Dramatic New Look at the Creative Roots of Science and Life*. Toronto, New York, London, Sydney, Auckland: Bantam Books, 1987.

Brandt, Deborah, and Carlos Freire (illustrator). *Naming the Moment—Political Analysis for Action.* Toronto: Jesuit Centre for Social Faith and Justice, 1989.

Campbell, Joseph. *The Immense Reaches of Outer Space: Metaphor as Myth and as Religion.* New York, San Francisco: Harper & Row, 1988.

Campbell, Peter, and Edwin McMahon. *Bio-Spirituality: Focusing as a Way to Grow.* Chicago: Loyola University Press, 1985.

Capra, Fritjof. *The Turning Point.* Toronto, New York, London, Sydney, Auckland: Bantam Books/Simon & Schuster, 1982.

Cardenal, Ernesto. *The Gospel in Solentiname* (4 vols). Maryknoll, NY: Orbis Books, 1982.

Colleran, P.K. *Walking With Contemplation: A Walker's Guide.* Berkeley, CA: CAFH Foundations, Inc., 1983.

Conlon, James. *Whatever Needs to Be Done.* Unpublished manuscript.
— *Emergings.* Unpublished manuscript.

Czerny, Michael, and James Swift. *Getting Started on Social Analysis in Canada.* Toronto: Between The Lines, 1984.

Diamond, Irene, and Gloria Feman Orenstein, Eds. *Reweaving the World: The Emergence of Ecofeminism.* San Francisco: Sierra Club Books, 1990.

Donovan, Vincent J., *The Church in the Midst of Creation.* Maryknoll, NY: Orbis Books, 1989.

Eisley, Loren B. *The Immense Journey.* New York: Random House, 1960.

Elgin, Duane. *Voluntary Simplicity: Toward a Way of Life That Is Outwardly Simple, Inwardly Rich.* New York: William Morrow & Co. Inc., 1981.

Feinstein, David, and Stanley Krippner. *Personal Mythology: The Psychology of Your Evolving Self.* Los Angeles: Jeremy P. Tarcher Inc., 1988.

Ferguson, Marilyn. *The Aquarian Conspiracy: Personal and Social Transformation in the 1980s.* Los Angeles: Jeremy P. Tarcher Inc., 1981.

Fifty Simple Things You Can Do to Save the Earth, Berkeley, CA: Earthworks Press, 1989.

Forest, James H. *Thomas Merton: A Pictorial Biography.* New York: Paulist Press, 1980.

155

Fox, Matthew. *A Spirituality Named Compassion.* San Francisco: Harper & Row, 1981.
— *Original Blessing: a Primer in Creation Spirituality.* Santa Fe, NM: Bear & Company, 1983.
— *Illuminations of Hildegaard of Bingen,* commentary. Santa Fe, NM: Bear & Company, 1986.
— *The Coming of the Cosmic Christ.* San Francisco: Harper & Row, 1988.

Fox, Matthew, and Brian Swimme. *Manifesto for a Global Civilization.* Santa Fe, NM: Bear & Company, 1982.

Freire, Paulo. *Education for a Critical Consciousness.* New York: Continuum, 1973.
— *Pedagogy of the Oppressed.* New York: Seabury Press, 1970.
— *Pedagogy in Process.* New York: Continuum, 1978.
— *The Politics of Education: Culture, Power & Liberation.* South Hadley, MA: Bergin and Garvey Publishers, Inc., 1985.

Freire, Paulo, and Antonio Ferendez. *Learning to Question: A Pedagogy of Liberation.* New York: Continuum, 1989.

Freire, Paulo, and Donaldo Macedo. *Literacy: Reading the Word and the World.* South Hadley, MA: Bergin and Garvey Publishers, Inc., 1987.

Gilligan, Carol. *In a Different Voice: Psychological Theory of Women's Development.* Cambridge, MA, and London: Harvard University Press, 1982.

Grof, Stanislav. *Realms of the Human Unconscious.* New York: E.P. Dutton & Co., 1976.
— *Beyond the Brain.* Albany: State University of New York Press, 1985.
— *The Adventure of Self-Discovery.* Albany: State University of New York Press, 1988.

Grof, Stanislav, ed. *Ancient Wisdom and Modern Science.* Albany: State University of New York Press, 1984.

Grof, Stanislav, and Christina Grof. *Spiritual Emergency.* Los Angeles, CA: Jeremy P. Tarcher Inc., 1989.
— *The Stormy Search for the Self.* Los Angeles: Jeremy P. Tarcher Inc., 1990.

Gutiérrez, Gustavo. *A Theology of Liberation: History, Politics, and Liberation.* Maryknoll, NY: Orbis Books, 1973.
— *The Power of the Poor in History.* Maryknoll, NY: Orbis Books, 1983.
— *We Drink From Our Own Wells.* Maryknoll, NY: Orbis Books, 1984.
— *On Job: God-Talk and the Suffering of the Innocent.* Maryknoll, NY: Orbis Books, 1987.

— *The Truth Shall Make You Free.* Maryknoll, NY: Orbis Books, 1990.

Hanh, Thick Nhat. *Being Peace.* Berkeley, CA: Parallax Press, 1987.

Hawking, Stephen. *A Brief History of Time: From the Big Bang to Black Holes.* New York, Toronto, London, Sydney, Auckland: Bantam Books, 1988.

Hays, Edward. *Prayers for a Planetary Pilgrim: A Personal Manual for Prayer and Retreat.* Easton, KS: Forest of Peace Books, Inc., 1989.

Hefner, Philip. *The Promise of Teilhard: The Meaning of the Twentieth Century in Perspective.* New York and Philadelphia: J.P. Lippencott Co., 1970.

Hope, Anne, and Sally Timmel. *Training in Transformation: A Handbook for Community Workers* (three vols.). Gweru, Africa: Mambo Press, 1985.

Hubbard, Barbara Marx. *The Hunger of Eve: One Woman's Odyssey Toward the Future.* Eastsound, WA: Island Pacific NW, 1989

King, Ursula. *The Spirit of One Earth: Reflections on Teilhard de Chardin and Global Spirituality.* New York: Paragon House, 1989.

Kolbenschlag, Madonna. *Lost in the Land of Oz: The Search for Identity and Community in American Life.* San Francisco: Harper & Row, 1988.

Kuhn, Thomas S. *The Structure of Scientific Revolutions.* Chicago: University of Chicago Press, 1990.

LaChapelle, Dolores. *Sacred Land. Sacred Sex. Rapture of the Deep: Concerning Deep Ecology—And Celebrating Life.* Silverton, CO: Finn Hill Arts, 1988.

Lakey, George. *Powerful Peacemanking: A Strategy for a Living Revolution.* Philadelphia and Santa Cruz: New Society Publishers, 1987.

Lindfield, Michael. *The Dance of Change: An Eco-Spiritual Approach to Transformation.* London and New York: Penguin, 1988.

McDonagh, Sean. *To Care For The Earth: A Call to a New Theology.* Santa Fe, NM: Bear & Company, 1986.

Merchant, Carolyn. *The Death of Nature: Women, Ecology, and the Scientific Revolution.* San Francisco: Harper & Row, 1980.

Merton, Thomas. *New Seeds of Contemplation.* New York: New Directions Publishing Corporation, 1972.
— *Seeds of Contemplation.* New York: Dell Publishing Company Inc., 1986.

Mische, Gerald, and Patricia Mische. *Toward a Human World Order: Beyond the National Security Straitjacket.* New York: Paulist Press, 1977.

Mische, Patricia. *Star Wars and the State of Our Souls: Deciding the Future of Planet Earth.* San Francisco: Harper & Row, 1985.

Muller, Robert. *New Genesis. Shaping a Global Spirituality.* New York: Doubleday, 1984.

Nouwen, Henri J. M. *The Wounded Healer.* Garden City, NY: Doubleday, 1972.

Perry, John Weir. *The Heart of History: Individuality in Evolution.* Albany: State University of New York Press, 1987.

Roszak, Theodore. *Where the Wasteland Ends: Politics and Transcendence in Postindustrial Society.* Berkeley, CA: Celestial Arts, 1989.

Russell, Peter. *The Global Brain: Speculations on the Evolutionary Leap to Planetary Consciousness.* Los Angeles: Jeremy P. Tarcher Inc., 1983.

Schaef, Anne Wilson. *When Society Becomes an Addict.* San Francisco: Harper & Row, 1988.

Schumacher, E. F. *Small Is Beautiful: Economics as if People Mattered.* New York: Harper & Row, 1989.

Shea, John. *Stories of God: An Unauthorized Biography.* Chicago: Thomas More Press, 1978.

Sheridan, E. F., ed. *Do Justice! The Social Teaching of the Canadian Catholic Bishops.* Toronto: Jesuit Centre for Social Faith and Justice, 1987.

Shore, Ira, and Paulo Freire. *A Pedagogy for Liberation: Dialogues on Transforming Education.* South Hadley, MA: Bergin and Garvey Publishers, Inc., 1987.

Soelle, Dorothee, with Cloyes, Sheily A. *To Work and To Love: A Theology of Creation.* Philadelphia: Augsburg Fortress Press, 1984.

Starhawk. *Truth or Dare.* San Francisco: Harper & Row, 1987.
— *The Spiral Dance: Rebirth of the Ancient Tradition of the Great Goddess.* San Francisco: Harper & Row, 1989.

Steindl-Rast, David. *A Listening Heart: The Art of Contemplative Living.* New York: Crossroad, 1983.

— *Gratefulness, The Heart of Prayer: An Approach to Life in Fullness.* Ramsey, NJ: Paulist Press, 1984.

Stevens, Anthony. *Archetypes: A Natural History of the Self.* New York:Quill, 1982.

Swimme, Brian. *The Universe Is a Green Dragon: A Cosmic Creation Story.* Santa Fe, NM: Bear & Company, 1984.

Tastard, Terry. *The Spark in the Soul.* London: Danton, Longman & Todd, 1989.

Teilhard de Chardin, Pierre. *The Divine Milieu.* New York: Harper & Row, 1960.

Terkel, Studs. *American Dream: Lost & Found.* New York: Pantheon, 1981.

Turner, Frederick. *Beyond Geography: The Western Spirit Against the Wilderness.* New Brunswick, NJ: Rutgers University Press, 1983.
— *Spirit of Place.* San Francisco: Sierra Club Books, 1989.

Van Matre, Steve, and Bill Weiler, eds. *The Earth Speaks.* Warrenville, IL: The Institute for Earth Education, 1983.

Walbek, Norman V. *Saving the Planet: The Politics of Hope.* Winona, MN: Northland Press, 1988

We find Conlon's book a significant synthesis of the personal, social, and planetary vision that must energize everyone concerned with the present devastation of the Earth and its peoples.

Ann Lonergan and Steve Dunn

Centre for Ecology and Spirituality

Conlon helps us navigate the passages among local, regional, global, cosmic—and come back home to local again. A guide through rough cultural and social seas.

Richard Harmon

Brooklyn Ecumenical Cooperatives

I am amazed at the breadth of *Geo-Justice: A Preferential Option for the Earth*. I am familiar with Tom Berry, Brian Swimme, Saul Alinsky, Paulo Freire, etc., but for the first time I see them all linked in an extraordinary synthesis. We are searching for a paradigm deeper and broader than the one in the past...

Desmond DeSousa

Federation of Asian Bishops' Conference
Office of Human Development, Philippines

Geo-Justice: A Preferential Option for the Earth presents the evolving paschal mystery story as experienced by the Earth. It challenges us, individually and collectively, to accept this process from death to resurrection. It guides our exploration through our social structure, our theology, our psychology, and our education.

Jim Conlon has eloquently presented a concept that empowers us. Through the pain of our death and labor of our birth, a "planetary Pentecost" is heralded in. *Geo-Justice* witnesses an awakening, and at the same time provides a tool to help others reflect upon the process evolving.

Jeneane Prevatt

Spiritual Emergence Network